THE
INDUSTRIALIZATION
OF RUSSIA
An Historical
Perspective

EUROPE SINCE 1500: *A Paperbound Series*

THE INDUSTRIALIZATION OF RUSSIA

An Historical Perspective

William L. Blackwell

NEW YORK UNIVERSITY

THOMAS Y. CROWELL COMPANY

NEW YORK / ESTABLISHED 1834

Preface

The purpose of this essay is to provide historical perspective in brief form on one of the most remarkable occurrences of modern times, the industrialization of Russia. It aims to make available to students and other interested readers the background usually lacking in more detailed and technical examinations of the contemporary economy of the U.S.S.R. It is not a survey of recent developments on the Soviet industrial scene: the focus will be on the transformation of Russia from agriculture to industry in the past century. The genre will be political and social history rather than economic analysis. The industrialization of Russia in both tsarist and soviet times is essentially, although certainly not exclusively, a study of state policy, of the state engaged in the mobilization of Russian society. Thus, government finances, political movements, bureaucracy, and war become as important for understanding its nature as factory production, entrepreneurship and labor, agriculture, transport, trade and technology. All will be brought into the discussion where they become essential to an understanding of the main theme.

Industrialization is a process which in most societies has involved the suffering, sacrifice, and waste of millions of lives. Russia did not avoid this misery, either in the tsarist or the soviet period. In approaching such a subject, scholars—historians and economists alike—have taken the most vigorous and antithetical positions. The thesis to be developed here, which is neither new, nor is it neutral, can be stated in the following general propositions. The industrialization of Russia is important to study because it differed greatly from that of Western countries. These peculiarities of Russian industrialization were determined very largely by the economic conditions, as well as the political and cultural traditions of Russia. Hence, to understand Russian, and particularly soviet, industrialization a broad historical perspective is required.

It is generally accepted among scholars that the process of industrialization encompasses at least four stages: the preindustrial, or traditional, society; a period of preparation in which the necessary conditions for rapid industrial growth are established; an industrial revolution; and the predominantly industrial society. Russian industrialization generally adheres to this pattern, although war, revolution, and despotism have altered many of the features, particularly of Russia's industrial revolution. Russia went through periods of political disruption which greatly impeded her industrialization, but she also experienced forced industrialization, which in turn had highly dislocating effects on the society as a whole. The organization of this essay will take into consideration both the general patterns and the peculiarities of Russian industrialization. Chapter 1 will provide a brief, introductory survey of the preindustrial Russian society of early modern times, of the factors which retarded and shaped industrialization, and the preconditions which were established from the seventeenth to the mid-nineteenth century for rapid economic growth. Chapter 2 will deal with the partial industrial revolution that took place in the last several decades of the tsarist period, the industrialization policies of the imperial ministers of finance, and the characteristics of Russian capitalism. Chapter 3 will consider the destructive impact of war and revolution on the Russian industrial economy during the years 1914–1921, the attempts of the soviet regime at industrial recovery during the NEP period, and the economic crisis that developed in the late 1920's. Chapter 4 will discuss at length the second industrial revolution engineered by Stalin; and Chapter 5 will conclude with a short summary of those aspects of industrialized Russia of the post-Stalin period that serve to complete the historical perspective.

The focus in each chapter is on how the rulers of Russia attempted to cope with the problems of backwardness peculiar to that country, the mechanisms of economic growth which they developed, to which I have referred—perhaps euphemistically—as the tsarist and Stalinist "methods" of industrialization. Each chapter will also contain a brief estimate of industrial growth in the period under consideration (or of industrial disintegration, as in the case of Chapter 3). I have not attempted precise or detailed economic measurements, but have deemed it sufficient in an historical survey of this type to give approximations based on more exact computations by economists. Reference to these studies will be made in both the text and the Bibliographical Essay at the end.

New York, New York   W.L.B.

Contents

1 / Preindustrial Russia

RUSSIAN TRADITION AND
RUSSIAN ECONOMIC BACKWARDNESS

In England by 1700 the conditions for industrialization had been set. The English industrial revolution was a dramatic beginning, but it was also the product of traditions and the culmination of processes traceable back into the middle ages: to feudal institutions; the decline of serfdom; the growth of towns, commerce, and a money economy as well as of agricultural production; the emergence of a middle class and a migrant, landless lower class; the appearance of national states; colonial expansion; rationalism, Protestantism, the emergence of new intellectual and moral values, and the development of science and technology.

Similarly, in Russia by 1700 a mold for industrialization had been created out of traditions and institutions the roots of which reached back for several centuries. However the path of Russian industrialization was to diverge sharply from that of England's. The pace was to be much slower; anything resembling the dynamism of the industrial revolution that began in England in the late eighteenth century did not manifest itself in Russia until at least another hundred years had passed.

What were the conditions that determined the uniqueness of Russian industrial development and why did Russia industrialize as late as she did? Essentially, there were three major problems, the seriousness of which diminished considerably, although

1

far from completely, as the industrialization of Russia gained momentum. They may be expressed very simply: Russia was big, Russia was poor, Russia was weak.

Geographical factors—Russia's size as well as her location—greatly impeded the industrialization of the country. Before the development of rapid land transport, it was difficult for the Russians to unite their mineral and fuel deposits, a necessity for the development of large-scale heavy industry. Effective and cheap transferral of these and other natural and industrial products to markets and ports was almost impossible in such a vast area without modern railroads and, to a lesser extent, canals. Natural waterways—the rivers, lakes, and seas—were largely isolated from the nation's resources, ports, and from each other, and were frozen over much of the year. In the summers of old Russia, caravans inched their way across the face of Asia following thousands of fleeting seasonal fairs. In the cold months, cargoes ceased to move altogether, except by sled. These primitive arrangements endured far into modern times. Until little more than a century ago, Russia had neither the warm water ports nor the rail junctures to provide the basis for permanent, urban markets. This meant that a modern commercial system to provide capital, credit, and markets for industrialization could not develop for most of her history.

Medieval Russia, established in the southern and western centers of Kiev and Novgorod, was a wealthy crossroads of world trade. In the thirteenth century, this situation changed dramatically. The crusades and the Mongol conquest severed ancient trade lines; control of commerce shifted west from Byzantium and the Baltic sea and passed into the hands of the maritime European states. Russia retreated from her former position of commercial eminence and wealth, to become for most of modern history an isolated northern kingdom, landlocked behind ice-clogged ports and hostile straits. The Russian navy, tardily developed, remained barricaded within inland seas. Since no Russian merchant marine was launched until most recent times, foreigners appropriated most of the country's external trade, on land as well as on sea. Russia had no gunboats or clippers, few merchant adventurers or conquistadors, and no pilgrims or black slaves. She could not acquire and develop overseas colonies. Although the tsars were hardly impoverished by the vast Asian and Slavic empire which they seized, the furs of Siberia, the cotton of Bukhara, and the grain of the Ukraine were a feeble capital when weighed against the vast treasures which flooded into London, Madrid, and Amsterdam from the European overseas empires. The European conquerers acquired large and profitable markets and the colonists built new and flourishing economies, both further enriching the mother countries. Russia appropriated endless unpeopled tracts of forest and desert; and her colonizing consisted very largely of unproductive agrarian migrations, or mass flights into the hinterlands, which depopulated and impeded the growth of the Muscovite home country.

The agrarian poverty of Russia presented formidable obstacles to industrialization and determined greatly the character of this industrialization. Poor soil in many areas, wastefully cultivated; large areas of swamp, desert, and other types of arid or frozen wasteland; long winters; dry summers; floods when the masses of snow and ice blanketing the plains suddenly melted; resources which were often difficult and expensive to exploit; and a sparse population, too small to adequately develop much of the land—all of these were major natural factors in determining Russia's extremely low level of agricultural production, which in turn moored the country in economic backwardness. The uniformity of natural conditions of the Russian and East European plain and the difficulty and expense of exploiting other resources made agriculture the main source of Russian wealth and at the same time severely limited this endowment. There was little possibility for the division of production and labor which would stimulate the growth of commerce, crafts, towns, and the middle classes; instead there was the perpetuation of a natural economy of dispersed wooden villages, migrations, and a low level of production. So long as agriculture constituted the main usable source of Russia's wealth, any large-scale economic development could be achieved only by the increased exploitation of an already impoverished peasantry.

The military weakness of Russia, together with her agrarian poverty, also worked both to create necessary conditions for industrialization and to fix the course of this industrialization. Russia, during most of the first millennium of her existence, was in a strategically indefensible position, located on the western end of the great plateau of forest and steppe which stretches—almost unbroken by mountain blockades of any real military significance—from Central Europe to China. She was surrounded on all sides by powerful and expansive peoples, politically and ideologically hostile, and was invaded and occupied many times. These military incursions from Asia and from Europe frequently resulted in economic disasters as well: prosperous cities were put to the torch; farmland was deserted amidst killing, enslavement, and flight to less fertile regions of the northeast. The only way that the new Muscovite Russia of this hard winterland could survive was to create a war machine inferior to none in Europe and Asia, a juggernaut which could roll back the military frontiers to a more defensible position. The needs of such a large armed force and the costs of an ambitious military imperialism for a country as poor as Russia were staggering. To meet these needs, the peasant masses were mobilized on a scale unprecedented in its rigor so as to procure through harsh sacrifices large shares of their produce. It was also necessary to create a permanent military serving class, as well as to impose stern discipline on other elements of the society. Such an exploitation of the peasants and regimentation of the elites in a large area consisting of thousands of dispersed villages could only be enforced by the most rigorous controls, backed by massive force. Only a leviathan state could effectively control all classes of the society. And thus it was that out of centuries of war and agrarian poverty, Russia had created by the beginning of her industrialization in the eighteenth century one of the most total despotisms of human history: a militarized state with a huge and cumbersome bureaucracy; a subservient church stripped of its lands; a servile but frequently treacherous nobility; a peasantry in bondage, occasionally erupting in aimless and bloody rebellions; and a line of autocratic rulers, some progressive and some reactionary, many spurred by megalomaniacal ambitions and paranoic cruelty, which often resulted in the increased impoverishment and suffering of their people. These factors greatly influenced the course of Russian industrial development. Industrialization would require an even greater mobilization of the people and consequent intensification of state control, but the methods had already been indicated for centuries.

At the same time, the Russian state retarded the development of conditions which would have facilitated an early industrialization along capitalist lines. The existence of the autocracy was directly related to the lack of social structure interposed between the state and the individual, and therefore to the absence of groups that could have assumed the tasks of industrialization. A middle class and a free, uprooted peasantry to provide managers and workers for factories did not appear in significant numbers in Russia until the nineteenth century. The same system that maintained the landlords in parasitic and unproductive leisure kept the peasant masses in poverty, ignorance, and servility, devoid of initiative and the capacity to produce at more than a very low level. Serfdom was more pervasive and long-lasting in Russia than in any other modern country. Similarly, the landlord and merchant classes were for generations tightly restricted by the state within a system of service and tax obligations, as well as being sustained by costly privileges. This prevented and discouraged the favored as well as the excluded from seriously pursuing competitive business enterprise.

The state controlled the church and through this institution was able to tighten its control over the people and the intellectual life of the country. In turn, it fell strongly under the influence of the antirational, antiscientific, xenophobic teachings of Russian Orthodoxy, which greatly discouraged the scientific development essential for the basis of industrialization. Contact with the cultural and scientific revolutions of the West was delayed for centuries. Although strong modernizing rulers, like Peter the Great, would succeed in minimizing the deadening effects of the old attitudes, at least among the small educated class, they could not insure against serious reactions, when obscurantist ideas in the hands of powerful bureaucrats might work to blight scientific development for generations. The illiteracy of the masses, particularly their technological ignorance, remained constant and unrelieved in a cultural situation where learning was considered politically and morally dangerous, particularly for the common people. In such a situation, only the development of a small, isolated, and persecuted circle of scientists limiting their research to highly abstract problems was possible. The result of this cultural dearth—combined with an almost total absence of the commercial conditions essential for the development and promotion of inventions—was long-term dependence on foreign technology, with all of the debilitating economic and political consequences flowing from such a dependence.

By the beginning of the eighteenth century, when the problem of industrialization first became apparent, it was clear that the immense and sprawling state apparatus which had grown in Russia lacked the training and flexibility to deal effectively with the complex tasks of stimulating, regulating, and managing industry. Superficial reforms had failed to eliminate deep-rooted traditions of corruption and favoritism. Personnel reaching up to the very top levels were illiterate. Administrative agencies had grown haphazardly with excessive duplication and overlapping of functions. Military personnel and methods were frequently employed for nonmilitary tasks. Harsh military discipline, the indiscriminate use of rigorous physical punishment, and heavy work quotas, imposed by brutalized local officials on captive peasant communities, were the ways by which production was maintained and resistance stifled. When such traditional military-bureaucratic methods of coercion would be transferred without modification to novel industrial situations, the frequent result would be low productivity, increased inefficiency, and desperate resistance, if not outright rebellion. Although foreign advisors would be imported, and foreign organization copied, it was the practices of the estate, the garrison, and the prison camp that would be applied in Russia's factories for many generations.

It was such a backward, impoverished, and despotic Russia that first squarely encountered, at the beginning of the eighteenth century, the modern great powers of Europe. By that time, these nations had achieved agricultural surpluses, great commercial wealth, an advanced science and technology, and all the social and political prerequisites for rapid economic growth. Capitalism, so impeded in Russia by a multiplicity of adverse historical conditions, flourished in Western Europe. The English industrial revolution was just around the corner. Russia's involvement in European power politics created both the crisis which stimulated her initial attempts to industrialize, and a dilemma which would haunt the Russian industrial effort through most of modern times. One of the ironies of Russian history is that Russia became imperialistic before rather than after her industrialization. Beginning in the early eighteenth century, Russia was subjected to a new and powerful pressure from the outside for rapid industrialization, in order to equalize militarily with the West. Each military defeat brought new incentives to modernize; but each military involvement with the advanced countries of Europe placed unbearable strains on a backward system. The dilemma of industrialization and modern war became critical for the tsars of the imperial period and fatal for the old regime. Such a dilemma was first faced by Peter the Great; but it was also Peter the Great who created the conditions for a stunted and belated capitalism to emerge in Russia.

THE PRECONDITIONS FOR INDUSTRIALIZATION

The industrial history of Russia, like most aspects of the modern history of that country, properly and dramatically begins with Peter the Great. Peter was the first ruler of Russia to develop and implement a systematic and comprehensive industrial policy. However, this does not mean that the complex problems of the origins and prerequisites for the initial economic growth of Russia can be understood by a perusal of his edicts. Before industry can appear anywhere, some foundation of capital, labor, technological improvements, managerial skills, and the means of distribution must be built. In Russia, this preindustrial accumulation of capital, or development of preconditions for rapid industrialization, as it is variously termed, was occurring at least several decades before Peter's reign, and continued for well over a century after his reforms, accelerated and stimulated by them.

By the middle of the seventeenth century, Russia comprised one of the largest political units in the world, a unified geographical entity, controlled by a powerful central government. The country had recovered from a series of devastating wars and rebellions; and invasion from hostile neighboring states or from Asia was no longer an immediate and dire threat. Most of Siberia had been acquired, and Russians were already beginning to exploit its wealth. There were stirrings of commercial life. Trade with western European countries had begun and a national domestic market was forming. Cities, such as Moscow, had become major commercial centers; and the precursor of one of the principal markets of the northern Asian land mass, what was later the Nizhnii–Novgorod fair, was functioning at Makarevsk.

Under such favorable conditions, the accumulation of capital, some of which could be diverted into primitive forms of industrial enterprise, was possible. Great landowners, such as the Morozov family, found it convenient and profitable to establish industries on their estates. Wealthy merchant princes—most famous among them the Stroganovs—not only bought land, but invested in mines and forges. The largest monasteries also sought to increase their wealth through manufacturing, as well as moneylending. Finally, the state itself did not hesitate to open its treasure chests in the pursuit of commercial and industrial wealth.

The most important Russian industries of the seventeenth century were agricultural, extractive, and military. No consumer market existed for manufactured goods; the state needed cannon and the church needed bells. For the rest, Russian industry was limited to those necessities that the earth could provide, and that the limited capital and technology of the estate could handle: distillation of liquor, manufacture of potash, and the mining of salt and iron. There were, of course, only a handful of shops and mines in pre-Petrine Russia, the most important of them concentrated in the Moscow region. Their existence signified not that the agrarian economy of old Russia as a whole was changing, but that resources and conditions existed for the development of industry. Land remained the primary form of wealth; the main economic concern of Russian entrepreneurs, whether nobles, merchants, or monks, was agriculture; the working force was almost exclusively made up of servile labor; and both technology and the means of transport remained primitive.

Peter the Great implemented a comprehensive state industrial policy for the first time in Russian history. A ruthless, imaginative, and dynamic leader, who thought big and acted decisively, Peter was well equipped to wield autocratic power effectively in the massive task of remolding a nation along Western lines. Nevertheless, he was not a revolutionary who wished to modernize Russian society, but rather a military reformer, interested in appropriating those Western techniques which would enable Russia to wage war successfully with European powers. However, such an updating of his armed forces required more far-reaching economic and cultural changes. Carried to their ultimate conclusion over a period of two centuries, Peter's reforms, by involving Russia in European civilization and power politics, would help to bring about the total transformation of Russian society from agriculture to industry. In his own time, military reform called for a far more modest, but important, chain of innovations. The army required supply industries and the improvement of transport. These in turn required the development of basic heavy industry. The new industry required workers and technologists; but these depended on scientific research, schools, and the tapping of new sources for managerial skills and labor.

Peter first began to build factories when war with Sweden cut off his primary supply of iron. By the end of his reign, over two hundred iron mills and other types of manufacturing enterprises had been built. Many of the mills were located in the Urals, an area rich in iron deposits and timber for fuel, although distant from the most important domestic markets, and even farther from the few ports through which Russia's high grade of iron could be exported. The cost of Russian iron thus was made prohibitive by transport costs and the proliferation of middle-men. This contributed to the decline of the Russian iron industry by the time of the European industrial revolutions. Peter was not interested in developing the iron trade, but in insuring iron production for his war machine, and he was willing to pay highly in terms of costs, loans, subsidies, and concessions.

Peter's first factories were built and operated by the state. Foreigners, who had dominated the tiny pre-Petrine industry, were discouraged. The new state industry proved insufficient to meet Russia's needs, and in the last half of his reign, the tsar used both coercion and money incentives to stimulate private industrial enterprise. By the time of his death, most Russian factories were in the hands of a small class of industrialists created by Peter from among his merchants and nobles.

It was far more difficult for Peter to find workers and engineers than to attract capitalists. He scraped the bottom of an empty labor barrel, using orphans, criminals, prisoners of war, and heretics. Ultimately, peasants owned by the state were consigned in perpetuity, or leased out, to factories. Slavery and industrialization thus went hand in hand in Russia's first effort to modernize. Technicians could not be conscripted; they had to be bought. Since industrial technology was nonexistent in Russia, Peter turned to Europe. But for the industrial effort he contemplated it proved insufficient simply to recruit foreign engineers and craftsmen, or to send Russians abroad to study technology. Ultimately, Russia had to build her own engineering schools, which in turn required the dual support of a system of elementary schools on the one hand, and centers for advanced scientific research on the other. All of this Peter recognized; and his educational reforms were crowned at the time of his death by the inauguration of the Academy of Sciences. However, all of this work was premature. For more than a generation Russia remained technologically illiterate, and her tiny school system a symbol rather than a working reality. Russian technological accomplishments were rare under Peter; perhaps the most important single work was the Vyshnii-Volochok canal system, which opened a maritime link between Russia's northern and southern rivers and seas. However, this engineering feat represented hardly more than an opening encounter with Russia's gigantic transportation problem; and not long after Peter's death, the weeds grew over his canals.

For a long time, historians believed that the post-Petrine period was one of economic stagnation. It was clear that the political situation had deteriorated; the government had slipped into the hands of dissolute women and foreign adventurers. So, it was reasoned, the hothouse industry created by Peter not only failed to grow, but fell into neglect when it was not plundered. These assumptions have been questioned by recent scholarship. It is now recognized that the Petrine tradition was continued, not abandoned, during the eighteenth century, although without Peter's dynamic leadership. Industry was fostered by Peter's successors, because it had become a political necessity to maintain his war machine. Russian industry grew.

There is no more striking example of this growth than the Urals industrial complex, founded by Peter. Peter's original twelve iron mills had expanded by 1790 to 165, many of them large enterprises, producing thousands of tons of iron each year. At the end of the eighteenth century, Russia was, with England, the world's leading producer of iron. However, this lead was soon far surpassed by the English, aided by the advanced technology of their industrial revolution. During the nineteenth century, the Urals industrial complex became a backwater.

Capable state administration was one reason for the growth of the Urals after the death of Peter the Great. Talented and energetic Russians, such as Vasily Tatishchev, and skilled foreigners of the calibre of the Saxon engineer G. F. Hennin (both hired by Peter), carried on the reformer's tradition. Private industrial enterprise was also an important factor in economic growth during the middle and late eighteenth century, both in the Urals iron mills and in other areas of the emergent Russian industrial economy. The Demidov family, in Petrine times Tula arms merchants, came to control a Urals empire of twenty-nine factories, employing thousands of serf workers. Proceeds from the sale of Demidov iron, the largest part of which was exported to England, brought the family over half a million rubles a year in the 1790's. Other merchant families invested substantially in Urals and Muscovite iron enterprises during the eighteenth century. An equally significant segment of the Russian metallurgical industry had passed into the hands of the Russian nobility by 1800. Many of these were court favorites or titled and wealthy entrepreneurial families of merchant origin, most notably the Stroganovs. Many landlords of lesser means sought to meet the increasing costs of a westernized way of life by building small factories on their estates. Liquor distilleries were a favorite type of noble enterprise in the late eighteenth century; serf labor, raw materials, and the few unsophisticated tools required, were all available to the small estate. Government protection and aid, which the noble entrepreneur had come increasingly to expect during the reign of Catherine the Great, did not, however, always insure against the ruin of badly managed undertakings.

There was no industrial revolution in Russia during the early nineteenth century, a time when several nations in Western Europe were undergoing rapid economic growth. Many Russian leaders were made painfully aware of this fact when their country, the foremost contender for the domination of Europe a generation before, was revealed in the Crimean War as an industrially backward, militarily second-rate power. This did not mean that the early nineteenth century was a period of economic stagnation for Russia. There were signs of a coming to life in many areas of the Russian economy during the reigns of Alexander I and Nicholas. I. Many of the preconditions for the more rapid economic growth of the late nineteenth century were established.

The Russian cotton industry experienced the most rapid growth, beginning in the second quarter of the century. There were many reasons for this, one of the more important being the industrial revolution in England, which provided cotton cloth cheap enough for Russian factories to import and print profitably. The ban on the export of English spinning machinery was lifted in 1842, enabling the Russians to make their own thread. The cotton industry was also able at a very early time to utilize the skills of Russian serfs trained in foreign mills located in the empire. Managerial skill and capital were provided by enterprising and thrifty serf craftsmen, the communal funds of Old Believers, and foreign industrialists and bankers. There was a limited peasant market for the coarse and relatively cheap Russian cotton fabric; and some of the same product could be sold in the Middle East and China. Thus, by 1850, a thriving industry, which was already modernizing its equipment, could be found in the cities of Moscow, St. Petersburg, and Ivanovo. By that time, Russia had become the world's fifth largest producer of cotton goods.

Other branches of the Russian textile industry remained essentially backward during the first half of the nineteenth century. Most of the heavy woolen cloth was manufactured for the army in primitive estate factories, although the worsteds industry, in the hands of middle-class capitalists and Old Believers in Moscow, was more progressive. Linen continued to be spun and woven in millions of peasant huts. The Russian silk industry was never of great significance in the prereform era.

Oil and coal remained largely unexploited in prereform Russia. The iron industry dropped from a position of world leadership to eighth place in global competition by 1860. The main reason for this decline was the high cost of Russian iron, which could not compete with the cheaper product of mechanized English mills. Russian iron was expensive because of the high costs of transporting goods vast distances on crude roads, or along slow moving and often unnavigable rivers and canals. The backwardness of Russian technology, combined with the weight of bureaucracy and the crude and wasteful exploitation of the labor force also contributed to the decline of the iron industry. Only a few big concerns were able to keep up with the times. The steel industry remained experimental; copper production was insignificant; and Russia's early leadership as a producer of precious metals was eclipsed by the gold rushes of California and Australia.

Although the Russian chemical industry was grossly retarded before 1860, as it continued to be during most of modern times, the machine construction industry, at least in St. Petersburg, experienced a modest beginning. Several large factories, which were developed by foreigners—Americans, Swedes, and Englishmen—were producing railroad cars, locomotives, and industrial machinery by the middle of the century. Few agricultural machines were manufactured in Russia before the soviet period; most were imported.

Of the agricultural industries, the manufacture of beet sugar became prominent during the second quarter of the nineteenth century, a technologically progressive industry, built on the estates of the great landed magnates of the Ukraine and the central Russian agricultural region. The manufacture of liquor, already significant in the eighteenth century, expanded at a very rapid rate in the succeeding fifty years. Russia became the world's greatest producer of hard liquor. Some vodka was processed in large, modernized distilleries, but most spirits came out of small and primitive estate stills, particularly in the Ukraine.

During the early nineteenth century, the population of the Russian empire increased rapidly, by about 60 percent or a total of almost seventy million people by 1863. Although the urban population grew at a faster rate than this, an insignificant number of people were concentrated in Russian cities and towns by the middle of the century, about 8 percent. However, the two capital cities were quite large, and had already begun the metamorphosis from administrative and religious centers to industrial hubs. A few new, more purely commercial or industrial towns were flourishing. Odessa and Ivanovo are the most striking examples of the new type, the first a thriving port, the latter a miniature "Russian Manchester" (as it was known at the time). Factories and working-class slums were being spawned haphazardly in the suburbs of Moscow, St. Petersburg, Riga, and other cities. By 1860, several hundred thousand men, women, and children labored in industrial plants. The majority of this new proletariat, however, were serfs who worked only seasonally with their masters' permissions. Much of the work was performed not at the benches of factories, but was farmed out to household shops. Outside of the few industrial centers cited above, most of the towns of Russia retained their traditional character before 1860: a church and parade ground, a few government buildings, a primitive marketplace, empty streets, and economic slumber.

Business institutions also were poorly developed in Russia before the last decades of the nineteenth century. In the pre-reform era, although there were a few wealthy court bankers who obtained loans for the government, and a larger number of moneylenders who bled the peasants, there were almost no commercial banks ready to lend money to industrial entrepreneurs or to invest in new business ventures. Most of the few state banks confined their operations to providing credit for landlords. Stock corporations were few and far between before the 1830's. At that time, new legislation opened the door slightly for some growth of this form of business organization. However, the instability of economic and monetary conditions in Russia—particularly the fluctuations of the paper ruble—were not inviting for the investor. The one exception to this stagnant situation was the rather rapid expansion of private insurance companies during the reign of Nicholas I.

There was a significant growth of both the foreign and the domestic trade of Russia during the early nineteenth century. Russian grain began to flow through Odessa to Europe; and European machinery and other industrial goods came back to Russia by several routes. Russia's trade balance remained favorable, at least on paper. However, the hidden costs of freight and smuggling (the former almost exclusively in the hands of foreigners) drained Russian treasure. England was Russia's biggest customer and merchant; and it was in English ships that most Russian goods were carried. However, Russian–American trade burgeoned during the early years of the nineteenth century: iron and hemp were exported, sugar and cotton imported. Russian industries, which soon exhausted the meagre domestic market consisting very largely of impoverished peasants, began to appropriate small foreign and colonial markets for textiles in the Middle East, the Ukraine, and China.

Commercial institutions remained backward in prereform Russia. Goods were sold for the most part at thousands of fairs which functioned for only a few weeks each year, usually in the summer. The beginnings of change were apparent by 1860; the big fairs were becoming less transient, their merchants less itinerant, and Russian industrial products were being marketed at the fairs in significant quantities. Large, permanent markets were being established in the more northerly cities. Halfway in an evolution from the oriental bazaar to the modern department store, the larger urban *gostinnie dvory* (merchants' markets, an old designation by which they were known) in Moscow and other important cities had become major commercial centers by the 1850's. At the same time, the *birzha*, or exchange, in St. Petersburg, established by Peter the Great, attracted foreign and Russian merchants, industrialists, and bankers for more sophisticated commercial and financial operations. Exchanges did not take root in other Russian cities and towns until much later; merchants continued to transact business in tea shops or on street corners in the traditional way.

The tsarist government never committed itself to a meaningful program for the industrialization of Russia during the early nineteenth century. Its primary commitment was to war and to the preservation of the existing social order. Although eloquent pleas were made in high circles for Russia to close the dangerous and rapidly widening economic gap with industrializing European countries, a mood of rigid conservatism generally prevailed in the tsarist bureaucracy. Departure from established budgetary procedures was viewed with alarm, particularly when the military allotment was questioned. The doors of the state treasury remained open to spendthrift landlords while business activity was not infrequently viewed as a suspect if not criminal manipulation. Factories were feared as politically dangerous concentrations of workers; and railroads were condemned as carriers of seditious foreign ideas.

The cost of war increased between 1800 and 1860 while state revenues remained limited. During the early nineteenth century, Russia became the "Gendarme of Europe" and a dominant power in the Middle East, but was obliged to support the heavy costs of her ambitious foreign policy with an archaic tax system. The bulk of tax revenue before 1860 was derived from the peasantry, directly through a poll tax, and indirectly through an excise on vodka. Little of the tax burden was shouldered by those who controlled most of Russia's agricultural wealth, the nobility. Much of the national income was squandered on luxuries and other forms of unproductive consumption by a few hundred of the wealthiest families. In part because of the inability and disinclination of the state to claim for itself a share of such a fertile reserve of capital, commerce and industry remained insufficiently developed to provide significant tax revenues.

Thus the state remained poor at a time when greater demands were placed on the treasury. The largest annual expenditure was that of the army and navy—rarely less than half of a budget that was always in deficit, even in peacetime. When Russia was at war, which most often was the case, military costs skyrocketed. From 1801 until 1856, the tsarist government was involved in several major and minor wars, frequently fighting with more than one country on more than one front at the same time. Russia invaded other countries many times and was herself invaded twice, with terrible destruction. Three major rebellions were crushed by the deployment of large Russian forces. Shaky thrones of Russia's allies were propped with millions of rubles. A depleted treasury could not meet the bills for these adventures, and the government resorted increasingly to borrowing at home and particularly abroad. When such costly loans did not meet the needs of war, unbacked paper money was printed in large quantities, adding inflation to the economic burdens of the tsars. On top of this Russia had to withstand the blows of frequent crop failures, and sometimes severe famines, for her basically agricultural economy was still dependent on the caprices of nature.

The strain of a major war with more modernized European powers was too much for the fiscal system of prereform Russia to withstand. Russia plunged recklessly into the Crimean War, deluded by past glories into believing that the obsolete army of an economically backward country could vanquish the more modernized industrial and military power of England and France. The Crimean War did not wreck the Russian economy, but it did bring the tsarist state to its knees in two years. Manpower reserves were exhausted, and the treasury was empty, as were the military warehouses. No more funds could be obtained by any means to meet the cost of an additional year of the most expensive war in Russia's history. Capitulation was necessary. This debacle shocked the Russian leadership into reform. It was a clear and urgent fact that Russia could no longer sustain modern war without industrialization. It was equally clear that involvement in modern war worked to impede industrialization.

Thus, although after 1856, industrialization became a primary concern for the tsarist regime, state industrial policy prior to this was haphazard and experimental. The government acted most forcefully during the early nineteenth century to improve the means of transport, so essential to the development of commerce and industry. Perhaps the main reason for official concern about transport, when other crucial areas of the economy were at the same time being neglected, was that rapid, efficient transport was a military as well as an economic necessity. This idea was foremost in overcoming the opposition of conservative officials to the construction of the first major Russian railroad—the St. Petersburg-Moscow line—built in the 1840's at state expense. Commercial considerations, however, together with the efforts of far-sighted and energetic administrators and engineers, were responsible for the completion of the several main canal systems of European Russia during the reigns of Paul I and Alexander I. Elsewhere, except for a few highways and postal roads connecting the main cities, Russians continued to plod through the dust, mud, and snow of ancient and unimproved trailways. On the rivers by 1850 only a few dozen smokestacks could be seen among tens of thousands of sails and the many barges, drawn by beasts and slaves.

In other important areas, where vigorous government intervention and initiative would have accelerated the industrial growth of the country, policy was feeble and regressive. Protective tariffs were maintained during most of the early nineteenth century. However, this was done as much to shield backward industries from competition as to develop new and progressive ones, or simply to increase revenues, even if this had a depressing effect on certain industries. The few state banks that came into existence were far from the coordinated national system of credit institutions equipped to provide ready capital for business ventures so desperately needed in many parts of Russia. The government did almost nothing to stimulate industry within the country or to attract foreign capital. The few primitive stock corporation laws of the prereform period were so rigid that frequently they were evaded. Some loans and subsidies were doled out to specific enterprises. However, this was more a matter of personal influence than official policy; and the total sum dispensed was a mere fraction of the vast funds the state placed at the disposal of landlords. Taxes and regulations excluded large segments of the population, particularly peasants, from business activities. There was no fundamental reform of Russia's unconvertible, unstable, and highly inflated paper currency, which deterred outsiders from investment risks. Thus, in most of the crucial areas of economic policy, the government approach was cautious and negative at best. For the rest, leading officials implemented inconsequential promotional schemes designed to impress on the tsar a concern for industry which was feigned, rather than plans aimed at truly stimulating its growth.

The private sector of the Russian industrial economy during the early nineteenth century showed far greater vigor than the bureaucracy. A clearly articulated industrial capitalism was in evidence by the 1820's and 1830's. Many of the great private industrial fortunes of the last decades of the old regime—of the Guchkovs, Konovalovs, Prokhorovs, Gunzburgs, Morozovs, and others—date to this period. The social origins of Russian capital and the way in which industrial capital initially was accumulated differed rather substantially from the patterns of early industrial capitalism in Europe. Although an increasing number of merchants began to invest in industry by the end of the reign of Alexander I, this source of industrial capital was proportionally smaller than in the West.

Religious outcasts, such as the Old Believers and Jews, were among the earliest of industrial capitalists and bankers in the tsarist empire, the former centered in the city of Moscow, the latter in the Ukraine and Belorussia. In both cases, business skills and capital developed not with the emergence of a capitalist mentality, but rather as the result of the persecution and restriction under which these groups lived. Such conditions fostered community cooperation, pooling of funds, the need for liquid capital, and involvement in business activities generally frowned upon, or forbidden to the servile or privileged orders of society. The Old Believer communities financed textile factories and employed co-religionists at their benches. The Jews accumulated capital through moneylending, the distribution of liquor, and the retail trade.

Foreign entrepreneurs began to make a contribution to Russian industrial development by the second quarter of the nineteenth century, although not on the scale of foreign control of Russian industry that was to develop by 1900. However, England, Scotland, the German states, France, Sweden, and the United States, the most important among several other nations, provided industrial entrepreneurs for Russia before the Great Reforms. Capitalists from the British Isles and the Germanies easily predominated, the former investing their technical skills, the latter their managerial and financial aptitudes.

The Russian landlord continued to build factories on his estates, as he had in the eighteenth century, as a way of meeting his pressing financial obligations. But these factories, despite the size of some multimillion-ruble industrial operations of notable families, such as the Yusupovs, were not essentially capitalist enterprises. Rather, they constituted outgrowths of the old despotic order, heavily subsidized, regulated, and protected by the state, and engaged in the supply of products for the army at fixed quotas and guaranteed prices.

A much more modern kind of entrepreneurship appeared during the early nineteenth century among peasants still in servitude. These were serf craftsmen and traders, who were permitted by their masters to engage in industrial and commercial ventures and to move to the cities, since this activity provided a new source of cash for the landlord. The peasant, for his part, had the legal protection of a noble. The most enterprising of such peasants began to build shops and factories. Some became wealthy industrialists, a few, millionaries. Thus, by the time of the 1861 emancipation, a small and influential class of peasant industrialists had come into being. The city of Ivanovo, Russia's first purely industrial municipality, originally a serf village belonging to Count Sheremetev, developed in this way.

All of these phenomena were evidence of important social and economic changes. Russian society was beginning to move relatively vigorously in the direction of industrialization. A foundation of capital and skills prerequisite for more rapid and comprehensive economic growth was being built. The state remained essentially backward in this process, clinging to a narrowly conceived idea of military modernization as sufficient for its needs. The shock of Russia's collapse in the Crimean War forced the leadership to embark on a more progressive course, and removed a major obstacle to comprehensive reform and more dynamic economic development.

2 / The First Industrialization Drive, 1856–1913

Russia under the last three tsars experienced a rapid, although partial, transformation from agriculture to industry, the main features of which are usually associated with an "industrial revolution." This first industrialization drive in Russia resembled in many ways the classic model provided by England in the late eighteenth and early nineteenth centuries. It was fundamentally a capitalist form of industrialization, with private enterprise, controlled in large part by Russian and foreign businessmen, playing a prominent role; financing through commercial banks and corporations; the rapid and early development of consumer industries; and the dislocation and pauperization of an urban factory working mass.

Important contrasts with English development should be noted. The role played by the state in tsarist Russia in stimulating and controlling industrial growth was unequalled in Western countries. Russia's industrial revolution was incomplete by 1913: crucial heavy industries remained stagnant or undeveloped, technology languished at a low level, and Russia remained dependent on the West for many of her machines and engineers. The factory working class was small and largely seasonal, while the peasant majority of the population was heavily taxed and exploited in other ways to serve the industrialization effort. Foreigners controlled a very substantial segment of private industry. This industry was highly concentrated in a few large complexes, the total product of which was small compared to the major economic powers of the West. By 1913, Russia was still more an agricultural than an industrial country; its wealth and people came from the villages more than from the cities.

Nevertheless, a remarkable economic growth took place in Russia during the last decades of the tsarist regime. By the eve of the Great War, Russia was the world's fifth industrial power. In terms of strict economic measurement, rapid industrialization began no earlier than the mid-1880's. However, the character of the Russian economy and society changed so rapidly in the preceding quarter century that one can in a broader sense fix the beginning of the industrialization drive in the late 1850's. A radical transformation of Russian society from agriculture to industry began actually with the social and economic reforms, the railroad building, the entrepreneurial awakening, and the vigorous fiscal policies of the era of the Great Reforms, although tangible economic results of many of the changes of the 1860's were not apparent until two or more decades later. It was a social and economic change both intensive and abortive when compared to the capitalist West. The cannon of the Crimean War announced the birth of Russian capitalism; those of the First World War sounded its death knell.

THE TSARIST METHOD OF INDUSTRIALIZATION

The industrialization of Russia that took place under the last three tsars, although prominently displaying many features of private capitalism, involved a far-reaching state participation and control, which was not as readily apparent. This control was far greater than that exercised by most European countries, although neither as total nor as direct as with the soviet industrial system. The tsarist government was not so much involved in the outright management and financing of industry (except in the case of railroads and a few other industries considered important to the state) as with more fundamental problems of the provision of capital and the creation of conditions which would engender and attract capital. However the primary method to which the tsars resorted, similar to their successor regime a generation later, was an exploitative one, involving the sacrifices of rural Russia's peasant masses for the benefit of the industrial sector of the economy. There was, to be sure, a fundamental distinction between the tsarist and soviet methods of industrialization beyond what was clearly a far greater degree of control exercised by the latter regime: the communist industrialization was in most respects autarkic. Except for the requisition of substantial technical assistance, the Soviet Union was relatively free of dependence on imports, as compared to tsarist Russia, which, by the beginning of the twentieth century, was closely bound to the world system of investment and trade. Such a distinction was, of course, not apparent to the Russian peasant. As far as he was concerned, Stalin's "first commandment" of 1931 to the collective farms, which obliged peasants to fulfill state quotas before all other dispositions of the crop, had been proclaimed by the tsarist Minister of Finance, Vyshnegradsky, forty years before, in the notorious dictum: "We may go hungry, but we will export!"

State industrial policy under the last three tsars may be divided into two phases, which correspond roughly to the patterns of economic growth of the period. The first phase extended from the end of the Crimean War to the mid-1880's. This period, which coincided in large part with the Great Reforms, was characterized by a new course in both industrial and agrarian policy, the general lines of which were continued until the First World War. Although these policies reflected a commitment to modernization which had not been apparent before, they also involved serious compromises and miscalculations which in the end helped to retard the economic growth of Russia. State industrial policies of the 1880's and 1890's were much more dynamic, reflecting not only more vigorous administration, but also the demands of accelerating industrial growth. Agrarian policies also became more positive in the last two decades of the century, but it was not until after the depression of the early 1900's and the political dislocations of the 1905 revolution that the government embarked on reforms geared to the removal of the major remaining impediments to industrialization in the Russian countryside.

The most significant event in the agrarian history of the reign of Alexander II was the emancipation of the serfs. The emancipation statute of 1861 represented a compromise of social interests, and at the same time a curious blending of the impulse to modernize and the wish to maintain the traditional agrarian order. It reflected a complex array of conflicting ideals and practical concerns: the need to secure Russia's position as a great power, abolitionist sentiment, and the fear of peasant revolution on the one hand; and on the other, the interest of the state in maintaining tight control over the peasantry for revenue purposes, the wish not to alienate the nobility, and the nationalist veneration of peasant institutions, for which there were eloquent proponents in both official and intellectual circles. The result was a limited agrarian reform which failed to create fundamental rural preconditions essential to rapid and comprehensive industrialization, but which in a number of other ways did stimulate economic growth. The peasant commune, together with the traditional practices of periodic repartition of divided strips of village land, and group responsibility for obligations, were retained. This kept most of the peasants in a state of semiservitude and immobility which retarded the formation of a permanent urban factory working force. It perpetuated the most backward and wasteful methods of farming. This, combined with the insufficient land settlement dictated by the reform and a rising birth rate, led to rural pauperization and a continuing low level of agricultural productivity. Because expanding urban populations could not be fed, and the cash crops were not large enough to provide adequate funds for massive industrial investment, a ceiling was erected over both the growth of cities and the accumulation of capital.

Nevertheless, the emancipation did mark a decisive break with the past; conditions were created for limited industrial expansion. The redemption system rechanneled the flow of rent obligations from the landlords to the government, where the funds could be more productively used. Since most of Russia's landlords had been heavily in debt to the government prior to 1861, vast funds which the peasants paid to redeem land from their former masters went in large part into the coffers of the state banks. The redemption payments, in addition to taxes, all of which were transmuted into cash obligations, forced the peasants to sell their crops and services to gain more and more money. This facilitated the growth of a money economy and rural grain markets, linked to Russia's ports by the new railroads. The emancipation also left the landlords with lions' shares of the land allotment. On these large estates, more grain could be produced for sale and export. Thus, despite the shortcomings of the 1861 agrarian reform as an instrument for radically increasing the efficiency of Russian farming and the mobility of the peasantry, a path was opened to industrialization. The serf emancipation, combined with the surge of railroad building to the grain producing areas in the 1860's and 1870's, provided the means for a unique method of state induced capital accumulation and industrialization through grain export and fiscal policy.

This method was first formulated by Alexander II's Minister of Finance, Count M. K. Reutern. By Reutern's time, the Ministry of Finance had become a powerful administrative unit with control over most of the agencies and areas of policy concerned with industrial development: the Treasury, the Mint, the State Bank, tariffs, state factories and mines, the regulation of many privately owned industries and business concerns, tax and monetary measures, and other specific matters of pertinence to economic growth. Most of the ministers of finance prior to Reutern's administration had been extreme conservatives or colorless bureaucrats incapable of vigorous implementation of policy. Beginning with Reutern, the calibre of these powerful officials improved. Reutern himself was highly trained in problems of state finances; and his successors for the remainder of the century, all capable men, had varied backgrounds in banking, engineering, and business management.

Reutern elaborated the essential lines of tsarist industrialization, which were adhered to until the last years of the old regime. This system began with a recognition of Russia's poverty and backwardness. Little capital could be derived, either from the poorly developed business community in Russia or from the government, the latter burdened with exhorbitant military expenditures and, at the same time, a primitive revenue system. The principal and very limited sources of revenue for the tsarist government, the head and liquor taxes extracted from the peasantry (although Reutern nearly doubled the former and regularized the latter), were grossly insufficient to finance both a military and an economic program of modernization. Neither of these programs could be sacrificed if Russia were to maintain national security and her position as a great power in the face of her defeats in the Crimean War and the emergence of a united German military-industrial goliath. Additional resources would have to be obtained. These could only come from outside Russia. An economic climate attractive to foreign investment and loans had to be created. Foreign bankers and investors would turn to Russia only when they believed that their investments were secure and profitable, and that their loans could be repaid. The problem, as Reutern correctly perceived, was at bottom a monetary one. No one would deal with Russia until there was faith in the stability of the paper ruble, or in the ability of the Russian government to provide bullion to meet its obligations to creditors. Russian paper currency, less than a century old in Reutern's time, had been chronically unstable during most of its short existence. Most recently, in the fiscal emergency of the Crimean War, the printing presses at the imperial mint had created inflationary chaos. The unconvertibility of the paper ruble was at the basis of its instability, and it had been kept in this condition almost all of the time since the reign of Catherine the Great because of erratic and capricious devaluations and the shortage of bullion. Russia's hidden and untapped mineral treasures could not provide the necessary minimum of precious metal; and a consistently passive trade and payments balance, because of dependence on European industry and shipping and heavy expenditures abroad, prevented an influx of silver. More frequently, it depleted the small stock of precious metal in the state vaults.

Since a substantial reduction in imports necessary to develop home industry would be self defeating, and a major curtailment of European expenditures by the nobility and the state was politically unrealistic, the only way that Russia could build up a bullion reserve sufficient to engender faith in the ruble was to increase exports to the point where the trade and payments balances became favorable. Europeans would never buy Russia's meagre, expensive, and inferior industrial products, although the Chinese and Persians and other oriental peoples might do so on a very small scale. The one thing that the Europeans, who constituted Russia's major market, would buy was grain—rye, oats, barley, but particularly, wheat. It was feasible by Reutern's time to build railroads to connect the wheat fields and rural markets with the Baltic and Black Sea ports; the large, commercial estates created by the emancipation were capable of producing for export; and the bulk of the peasantry would be forced to sell rather than consume substantial portions of their grain crops to meet increased tax obligations and the new burden of redemption payments. If, through these severe measures, a high level of grain export sufficient to create a favorable trade balance could be maintained, Russia's stock of bullion would grow and the stability of her currency would be assured. Massive foreign investment would be attracted to Russia, facilitating the growth of railroads, industries, and cities and preserving the empire's international power and prestige.

The basis of this system was exploitation of the peasantry. The penalties which the peasant faced for evasion of his substantially increased taxes were confiscation of personal property or barbaric whippings. Hardly able to produce enough to feed himself on a small and inadequate plot of land, his soil ravaged by backward agricultural methods, he now had to neglect his health through overwork, liquidate his livestock, and cheapen his diet, and yet produce his surplus for the state. He was exposed to the vicissitudes of nature and of the marketplace. A crop failure or a drop in the international price of grain (and with the latter, he had to face increasingly the price competition of the bountiful and more efficient farms of the United States) brought no relief in the government's exactions and hungry days to the village. A famine could bring death to millions.

The financial strains of such a natural disaster, or the heavier burden of war preparations and expenses, also could easily collapse such a fragile financial mechanism; and we find most of the ministers of finance under the last three tsars leaving office under the shadows of such crises. There simply wasn't enough wealth generated to deal with extraordinary situations. Reutern himself very probably overestimated Russia's capacities. He attempted convertibility at the beginning of his administration with insufficient bullion reserves. These stocks were soon rapidly depleted, and unconvertibility had to be restored the year after the initial reform. Thereafter, Reutern contented himself with building a silver reserve sufficient to meet prompt dividend and interest payments in bullion to foreign creditors and investors. He did this by floating loans in Europe. European bankers charged high rates for undertaking such risks, with the result that a huge debt accumulated. Frequently, the annual carrying charges on this debt exceeded what could be borrowed at the same time. In addition to this fiscal millstone, Reutern piled onto the Russian economy the burden of lower tariffs, which cut revenues and increased imports. The end result of the new system, which included significant administrative housekeeping reforms and measures to develop credit institutions in Russia, was a fiscally precarious and costly method of industrialization, but one which worked and which stimulated a moderate economic growth in the 1860's and 1870's.

More dynamic industrial and agrarian policies were instituted by the tsarist government in the 1880's. These reflected in part the administration of Nikolai Bunge (1881–1887), a trained economist and banker. They also marked a response to the quickening growth of the industrial economy and, simultaneously, a sharpening agricultural crisis. Bunge's policies were more ambitious than those of Reutern—he wished to attack the task of industrial growth and the problem of rural poverty at the same time—but, like his predecessor, he overestimated the capacities of Russia's backward economy for rapid growth and generation of wealth. Bunge was not a visionary, nor was he a liberal. A practical-minded official, the aim of his agrarian policy was not so much to help the peasant increase his income as to industrialize Russia through increasing the peasant's capacity to produce.

This involved lightening the tax load. It was Bunge who was instrumental in abolishing the ancient salt tax; more important, toward the end of his ministry, the burden of the head tax was lifted. Bunge's reforms reduced direct tax payments from Russia's villages by over a third. Although the purchase ("redemption") of land allotted for sale to the peasants by the 1861 Emancipation Act was made mandatory, increasing the government's income from the countryside, the scale of these payments was soon reduced. Bunge's policies thus represented a substantial easing of tax pressures on the peasant. Credit was also eased through the liberal lending program of the Peasant Land Bank, opened in 1883.

Bunge's program aimed at developing the rural economy through the infusion of state capital and the shifting of taxes away from the peasants. To bolster the depleted state revenues, he levied sales taxes, directed at the more affluent consumer groups, on sugar, oil, tobacco, and, most notably, property transfer. Tariffs began once again to climb, with a positive effect on Russia's trade and payments balances. The government began to acquire and build railroads as a way of cutting costs and accumulating revenue through freight charges and fares.

Although Bunge's policies in the long run would have been less wasteful and exploitative than those of his predecessors, they were costly at the beginning when funds were scarce. Russia could not yet afford to pay for them, the budget could not be balanced, and Bunge had to borrow. Confidence in the ruble was further shaken by the expenses and the fears engendered by Russia's imperialist adventures in Bulgaria and Central Asia. The fiscal problems which Reutern had somewhat alleviated were returning.

Bunge's successor, Ivan Vyshnegradsky, an engineer, business executive, speculator, and a tough conservative, saw the remedy for Russia's economic ills, not in borrowing or in tax and interest cuts, but in the more austere disciples of sacrifice and saving. The keystone of Vyshnegradsky's "system" (as it was called) was gold hoarding. This was done primarily through increasing grain exports. The sale of grain, in turn, was forced by raising taxes. Sales taxes on kerosine, beer, and vodka—all consumed heavily by the peasants—were levied. The collection of long standing arrears on direct taxes (poll, land, and others), as well as on redemption payments, was prosecuted rigorously at times when grain prices were low, so as to increase export crops. Shipping rates for grain on the railroads were cut. High taxes also worked along with the grain export policy to create favorable trade balances. Tariffs, along with revenues from newly acquired or constructed railroads, helped to balance the budgets. Interest on foreign-owned bonds was cut by the negotiation of more favorable loans from competing European markets.

Vyshnegradsky's system filled the treasury (the gold reserves more than doubled), but it impoverished the rural economy. Both the pockets and the grain bins of the peasants were emptied. Just as Bunge's program had left the state treasury unequipped to meet the burden of war, Vyshnegradsky's policies left the countryside unable to withstand a crop failure. The famine of 1891 brought mass starvation to the provinces, and soon after, Vyshnegradsky's fall from power.

The most famous of the tsarist ministers of finance was Sergei Witte, who is usually given credit for the industrial boom which took place during the period of his administration (1892–1903). Witte, also of a business background like Vyshnegradsky, actually continued his predecessor's basic policies without drastic innovation. He reaped both the benefits and the curses of the Vyshnegradsky system. The difference was in the man: Witte envisioned a major modernization effort, and was a much more vigorous administrator than his predecessors or successors. It was Witte's realistic perception and passionate conviction that to maintain the power and prestige of Russia as a world leader, the state had to promote a much more rapid industrialization than had previously been its policy. Only such a big push would release the resources and energies of the country for sustained economic growth of a capitalist type, and end Russia's dependence both on nature and on the industrialized powers. Like Bunge, Witte realized that such growth was not possible in the long run, unless Russian agriculture was nurtured and expanded rather than bled. However, although Witte eventually became a partisan of fundamental agrarian reforms along the lines of the subsequent Stolypin laws, he was never able or willing to give first priority to agriculture during his term as Minister of Finance. He very probably would have come to this, had he not been dismissed after the depression of 1901–1903. As he was often accused, like his predecessors, Witte overestimated the capacities for dynamic change of Russian society.

Thus, as with Vyshnegradsky, favorable budgetary and trade balances were maintained through massive grain export, higher taxes, state acquisition or construction of railroads, and high tariffs. This was designed to bring about fiscal stability and to facilitate Russian borrowing abroad as well as foreign investment in Russia. In most of these policies, Witte went a long step beyond his predecessors. Not content with the purchase of privately owned railroads, he plunged into the mammoth project of the Trans-Siberian line. Following Vyshnegradsky's beginning, Witte not only vastly augmented Russia's gold reserves, but was able to introduce by 1898 a convertible gold currency system. Not only were sales taxes raised, but a government monopoly on the distribution of vodka was imposed, a measure which substantially increased revenue. Under Witte, massive loans were floated in Europe, until Russia had the world's largest foreign debt. As a result of Witte's policies, there was also a major infusion of foreign investment. Taking a broader view of economic growth than his predecessors, who tended to become absorbed in fiscal or agrarian problems, Witte worked to develop commercial independence for his country through a Russian merchant marine, and invested large sums of money in technical education.

Despite such achievements, Witte's policies, in their neglect of the peasant, aggravated the problem of land reform. How long could a fundamental agrarian reorganization be postponed? How many years could the Russian village be bled, before the exhaustion of productive capacities and peasant discontent would precipitate a major crisis in the countryside? It was obvious by the beginning of the twentieth century that rural Russia was descending into an economic and political catastrophe. Russia's agrarian problems were clearly articulated by a growing number of economists critical of the Witte system; rural political difficulties were enunciated more dramatically by the frequency of peasant riots. Twenty million peasants were starving after a half decade of Witte's policies, his critics charged. Their accusations were not without foundation. It became increasingly apparent that, not only were the tax-paying powers of the *muzhik* exhausted, but the fertility of his land, to say nothing of his own physical stamina, were being sapped away. As the rural population expanded rapidly and the government forced ever higher exports, grain prices and wages fell, and the peasant's debts, tax arrears, and rent obligations mounted. His cattle were sold; his vegetable gardens and pastures turned over to grain. Without livestock, he was deprived of a primary source of food, fertilizer, and power. Insufficient land, exhausted and eroded soil, and a deteriorated diet marked the beginning and end of a road of despair. Such hopeless conditions produced violence, riots, burnings, and pillage on a very large scale, particularly during the last years of Witte's administration. By 1905, the government had to face peasant rebellions, the scope and ferocity of which recalled the jacqueries of the time of Pugachov.

The government's immediate reply was rigorous armed intervention. By 1906, these reprisals had reached the proportions of a massive military pacification of the countryside. Order was restored; but the frightening experience of intensified peasant violence of the previous several years had the cumulative effect of pushing officials from what had been no more than experimentation with new types of peasant land tenure into the most significant agrarian reforms of the tsarist period.

It will not be pertinent to the subject at hand to detail the complex legislation spanning the years from 1903 until 1911, which is identified as the Stolypin reforms. The main intent of these laws was to liquidate the powers of the commune over the peasant, to eliminate restrictive communal institutions, such as periodic repartition and mutual responsibility, and to establish a system of permanent, individual ownership of consolidated plots of land. The end result would be the establishment of a free, rural middle class on the ruins of the old slave society of communalized state producers. The impact of such a far-reaching social reform for the industrialization of Russia was not uppermost in the minds of the reformers. Although they were not opposed to modernization, political considerations were their primary concern. What changed the thinking of most of Russia's gentry and officialdom by 1905 (including the forceful leader Peter Stolypin and his collaborators) was the realization that only by giving the peasantry a vested interest in the existing order could revolutionary violence and destruction of property be minimized and stability restored to Russian society. Nevertheless, the reforms of the period 1903–1911 worked to increase agricultural production for purposes of export and the urban food supply, to alleviate peasant land hunger, to expand the rural market for Russian industrial goods, and to facilitate the migration of labor to the cities.

In the broader context of the economic growth of Russia, tsarist policy after 1905 was hardly stagnant. In some fundamental ways, it was more dynamic than the programs of Witte and Vyshnegradsky. Its effect, not wholly intended, was to encourage the growth of capitalism, not only in the already rapidly industrializing Russian cities, but in the primitive countryside as well. This was accomplished, not only through the primarily fiscal measures employed by the finance ministers of the late nineteenth century, but by promoting a profound change within peasant society itself. The same reform from a political point of view was also deeply conservative, designed as it was to encourage individualism, to foster the institution of private property, and to prop up the existing order, while at the same time creating new classes of impoverished and propertyless factory workers and peasants. As a result, new social tensions as well as new economic forces were created. Both would have a marked effect on Russia's subsequent industrialization.

RUSSIAN CAPITALISM AND FOREIGN ENTERPRISE

Another very immediate economic problem posed by tsarist policies of the late nineteenth and early twentieth centuries was that of Russia's potential for rapid capital accumulation. Here was the unknown quantity that the finance ministers of the last three tsars had found so difficult to gauge. Would a Russian capitalist economy—capitalist institutions, banks, insurance companies, entrepreneurial incentives and skills—generating wealth sufficient for accelerated economic growth, necessarily and immediately be the result of the strenuous system of state stimulation and control of industry that Witte and his predecessors had developed? Even should this be the case, there loomed the long range problems of debt payments and power politics arising from the dependence on foreign capital and technology that tsarist industrialization methods presupposed. What forces were at work and what policies could be developed to diminish this costly dependence on the money and techniques of others and to check the advance of European and American imperialism?

During the last three decades of the tsarist period, there was a very rapid development in Russia of financial institutions and types of industrial organization characteristic of the more advanced capitalistic economies of Europe and the United States. Such development in Russia was both less extensive and more intensive than in the West. There was a great degree of concentration of industry and banking in very large corporations in the main cities, but very little spreading of financial and industrial activity to smaller towns and to rural areas. By the beginning of the First World War, most of Russia's metallurgical industry had merged. A tendency toward monopoly was also to be seen in the textile, fuel, and transport industries.

By the 1880's, both state and private banks began to play a major role in the industrialization of Russia. The state banking system was extensively reorganized by the finance ministers of the last three tsars. Although the traditional interest of the government in lending money to the nobility was continued by the creation of a new Land Bank, other state agencies were created which could provide capital for industrial development. The maturation of Russian industrial capitalism as well as tighter financial bonds with Europe were reflected in severe and prolonged economic crises in the early 1870's, again in the 1880's, and very sharply, at the beginning of the twentieth century. In the same year, the State Bank, established in 1860, operated 982 branches. The State Bank functioned not only as a savings and loan institution, but also as a central state agency for the coordination of currency and the facilitation of business transactions. In times of economic crisis, it acted as a prop for the banking system as a whole.

While building a state banking system, the tsarist government encouraged the growth of private banking. Practically nonexistent in Russia before legislation of the 1870's, thousands of private banks and their branch offices were established during the next half century. Most of these were small municipal banks, mutual credit societies, and cooperatives formed by peasants, craftsmen, and landlords. They provided mainly mortgages, as well as credit to merchants and petty entrepreneurs. The most important source of capital for Russian industry by 1914 was the forty-three corporative commercial banks, with their several hundred branches. These were the giants of Russian finance, which provided loans and credit to industrialists in the late nineteenth century, and in the last two decades of the tsarist period turned increasingly to direct investment. The tendency toward concentration characteristic of capitalist industry in Russia during this final phase can also be seen in the area of private banking. By 1914, the ten largest commercial banks were worth over one half billion rubles. About half of this capital had passed into the hands of foreigners, for the most part, French investors. Trading was done very largely in the stock exchanges of St. Petersburg and Moscow, which had assumed by the turn of the twentieth century major importance in the Russian financial world.

The industrial growth of the late tsarist period both prompted and was stimulated by the development of private insurance. Here, as we have seen in other areas of Russian capitalism in the last decades of the old regime, there was a marked tendency toward consolidation. By 1910, almost thirteen billion rubles' worth of property was insured by a dozen large corporations. Most of these corporations had been founded in the 1850's and 1860's. This formative period of the Russian insurance business was one of cutthroat-rate competition. The last quarter of the nineteenth century saw the emergence of coordinated pricing efforts among the major insurance concerns, as well as the introduction of more scientific statistics. During the same period, foreign insurance firms established branches in Russia. The Russian companies, for their part, began to sell insurance in Europe and the United States. Russian insurance companies were permitted a relatively free hand in investment matters. They were able to provide substantial capital for various industrial undertakings in their own country, particularly the railroads.

A class of capitalist entrepreneurs, which had already emerged in Russia during the last decades of serfdom, became an important economic and political force by the first decade of the twentieth century. A large part of the industrial capital was concentrated in several hundred very large firms. In addition, there were thousands of much smaller privately owned commercial and industrial enterprises. Big business began to organize extensively by the turn of the century, and played a vigorous role in the Russian political parties that came to life during and after the 1905 revolution.

Russian-born capitalists tended to dominate in consumer industries: textiles and particularly woolens manufacture; the sugar processing industry; and the production of kerosine. Entrepreneurs of Russian extraction very largely controlled domestic commerce and the private sector of the railway network. Much of the control of other heavy industries, however, had passed into the hands of foreign entrepreneurs and investors by 1900. This was particularly true of steel and oil, less the case with foreign trade, banking, and insurance.

If one wished to identify, in Portal's phrase, the "truly Russian industrial bourgeoisie," then one would turn to Russia's ancient capital and center of Russian nationalism—to Moscow, and to the Muscovite textile industry. Here, many of the descendants of the Old Believers who had helped to found the industrial life of that city now controlled most of its factories, shops, banks, exchanges, business organizations, and its political life. In a century's time, these cotton and woolens industrialists had accumulated a vast capital in primarily family enterprises. As a consequence, they were hardly dependent on the bankers of St. Petersburg or of Europe. Intensely nationalistic, they formed an elite of powerful families, and by the twentieth century began to view themselves as the political and cultural, as well as economic, leaders of the nation as a whole. The Guchkovs and Konovalovs went into national politics; the Ryabushinsky's, Botkins, Tretyakovs and Alekseyevs both patronized the sciences and arts and made creative contributions as well. Symptomatic of the clash between tradition and change characteristic of the times, of the parvenu qualities of the new ruling class, and of the decrepitude of its inheritance, the Prokhorovs joined the nobility less than a decade before the revolution; while the famous Savva Morozov, heir to one of the greatest Russian industrial fortunes, supported a socialist movement that hardly had been born.

Elsewhere in industrializing regions of the Empire, Russian entrepreneurs mingled and competed with Russianized, semi-Russianized and un-Russianized businessmen of many national origins. In the western provinces, a small but influential Jewish *haute bourgeoisie* had emerged from poverty-stricken ghettos. Their headquarters were the big commercial and financial centers of Russian Poland and the south: Odessa, Berdichev, and Warsaw. Most prominent among this group of Jewish entrepreneurs were Ivan Bloch and Samuel Poliakov, the "Railroad Kings"; the Gunzburgs, bankers of international repute; the "Rothschilds of Russia," who were at the same time leaders of the

Russian Jewish community; Dembo and Kagan, the kerosine monopolists; and sugar barons, most notably Israel Brodsky, whose stores were spread throughout the tsarist empire. Brodsky competed with an emergent bourgeoisie of Ukrainians enriched by the sugar industry, such as the Tereshchenkos. Western European entrepreneurs also figured largely in the industrialization of the Ukraine. There is no more outstanding example of this intrusion than the Welsh industrialist John Hughes, who brought capital, techniques, and even workers from Wales and England to build a large and modern center for the Ukrainian steel industry at the town then named after him, Yuzhovka.

The European, Ukrainian, and Jewish capitalists of Russian Poland had counterparts of other nationalities in various parts of the empire, most notably the Germans of the St. Petersburg–Baltic area. These Germans enjoyed many more privileges than the other national minorities, and were quickly absorbed into the upper levels of the Russian social-economic structure and business community. In Riga, they controlled the economic life of that rapidly industrializing city. Germans, like the first "kings" of the 1860's and 1870's, Von Meck and Von Derviz, built railroads; Germans, like Baron Stieglitz, were the first big bankers in Russia; Germans, like the famous Ludwig Knoop, were the first big financiers and managers of Russian industry.

The home base of many German merchants and bankers was St. Petersburg. Retaining its significance as one of Russia's greatest ports and industrial towns, it was also assuming by 1900 the role of financial center for the empire. Here, banks played a major role in the provision of capital and the formation of large corporations and trusts that were becoming more characteristic of Russian industrial life. The financier-industrialist type was making his appearance in Russia with the coming of the Putilovs and Vtorovs, although on a much less spectacular scale than the Goulds and Morgans of America. Foreign control was more prominent in St. Petersburg than in other Russian industrial cities. The business community assumed more and more a cosmopolitan flavor. The English remained prominent in the city's textile and machine industries; and there were increasing ranks of wealthy

Swedish, French, German, and Belgian industrialists and bankers. A few American firms were becoming an economic force in St. Petersburg, particularly in the insurance business.

Thus, despite the emergence of a native capitalist class, Russia by 1914 remained heavily dependent on the foreign entrepreneur. The foreigner brought technical and managerial skills still in critical shortage, and which Russia still could not herself supply sufficiently. The dependence of Russia on foreign capital and technology intensified rather than slackened in the period 1890–1914. This was both a cause and a consequence of the accelerated economic growth of the period. In the half-century from the emancipation of the serfs to the First World War, the proportion of foreign investments in Russian corporations went from 13.4 percent to one third. Even in the traditionally Russian cotton industry, a fifth of the capital was foreign; and nearly a third of the largest factories were entirely controlled by foreigners, who also owned almost all of the domestic cotton crop. Similarly, the Caucasian oil and Ukrainian coal and metallurgical industries were very largely in the hands of foreigners. A third of the capital in the big commercial banks was foreign. Foreigners controlled the largest parts of the embryo electrical, chemical, and machine industries. They were least influential but still played a role in woolens manufacture, insurance, and maritime navigation.

Russia became increasingly dependent on foreign technology during the last half-century of the old regime. This type of foreign influence cannot be measured as precisely as the number of enterprises, stocks and bonds owned by Europeans and Americans, but a definite pattern of technological backwardness and dependence can be identified. Paradoxically, the number of technical schools on all levels increased significantly, and the quality of these schools improved in the post-Reform period. Government support for technical and scientific education was generous, particularly after the 1880's. Outcroppings of official obscurantism never seriously impeded scientific development, and had no significant effect on the progress of applied science and technology. By 1900, with a tradition of two centuries of experimentation at home and close contact with developments in the West, Russian science had reached a high level of sophistication and enjoyed world esteem. This was particularly true of mathematics and many of the physical sciences. The towering figure of Mendeleyev indicates the progress Russia had made in the scientific world by the time of the famed chemist's death in 1907.

With such a theoretical and educational foundation, it is not surprising that Russian engineers, technologists and inventors of genius and distinction made their appearance. The study of the generation and application of electric power, for example, a tradition extending back to E. K. Lenz and B. S. Jacobi at the Academy of Sciences in the 1830's, was renewed in a European setting at the end of the century with the work of Yablochkov and Dolivo-Dobrovolsky. At the same time, however, the history of technological innovation of a generation before repeated itself, if on a more sophisticated level. Russian inventors created telephones, radios, motion picture cameras, light bulbs, internal combustion engines, airplanes, and tanks, simultaneously with, and in some cases earlier than, Europeans and Americans. However, there was little state-sponsored or commercial innovation of this technology. Russia continued to import most of its machinery and equipment, which was the cheaper and safer thing to do. Foreign firms—Hughes' New Russia Steel Company, Bell Telephone, Singer Sewing Machines, International Harvester, among many others—built new and larger factories and installations in Russia. The seizure of these factories and other foreign assets was easily accomplished soon after the Russian Revolution; it was a more difficult task to cut the lifeline of foreign technology, upon which Russia continued to depend heavily for more than a generation.

INDUSTRIAL GROWTH

Some relatively substantial estimates of Russian industrial growth under the last three tsars have been made, despite the paucity of statistics, particularly before the 1880's. Although certain sectors of Russian industry, particularly cotton manufacture, expanded very rapidly in the 1860's and 1870's (continuing a trend that had been clear even in the last decades of serfdom), a rapid and at the same time quantitatively significant industrial growth can not be seen until after 1885. In 1887, total industrial production was estimated (in official figures) at 1,334,500,000 rubles; for 1900, we have another estimate of 3,005,000,000 rubles; and in 1913, Russian factory inspectors set the gross output of Russia's industry at 5,621,000,000 rubles. In 1860, total industrial production is estimated to have been about a tenth of the 1913 level. In 1885 (when the figures become more precise), 20.57 percent had been achieved; in 1900, 61.05 percent, and in 1910, 83.88 percent. This represents an average annual rate of industrial growth during the period 1885–1913 of 5.72 percent, with a peak of 8.03 percent in the 1890's and a low of 1.43 percent in the years of depression and revolution in the first half decade of the twentieth century.[1] Such a rate of growth was not phenomenal when compared to Sweden, the United States, and Japan in about the same period, or the Soviet Union in the early 1930's, but it is clear evidence that Russia was undergoing in the 1890's the fundamental economic change or "take-off" that is associated with an industrial revolution.

However, several peculiarities of Russian industrial development in the late tsarist period should be noted. First, the ratio of agricultural to industrial production continued to favor the former. By 1913, the value of industrial production was just less than half that of agriculture. The expansion of agricultural production was much slower than that of industry, retarding the overall growth rate. On the eve of World War I, half of the value of industrial output was derived from consumer industries (textiles foremost and food industries second). Little more than a fourth was produced by mining, metallurgy, and machine construction. Despite a concentration of factory industry unequalled anywhere else in the world, almost a third of the total value of Russian industrial production on the eve of the First World War

[1] Gershenkron's figures. See Bibliography.

was still derived from small shops and peasant cottages. Real per capita income remained very low in tsarist Russia, about equal to that of Italy, and far below the levels attained by the advanced industrial powers of the West.[2]

New industrial regions developed in Russia after 1861. The bulk of Russian industry was still centered in the three areas which had developed during the early nineteenth century. Foremost were the several provinces around Moscow, which accounted for over a third of the industrial production of the empire at the end of the nineteenth century. Moscow remained the textile center of Russia. Another third of the total industrial production was concentrated in the province of St. Petersburg and the Kingdom of Poland. Russia's earliest industrial center, the Urals, continued its decline, providing about 5 percent of the gross industrial output. The Ukraine replaced the Urals during the late nineteenth century as a center of heavy industry. Ukrainian mining and metallurgy, together with the valuable beet sugar industry, accounted for a fourth of Russian industrial output by the 1890's. The remaining fraction of industrial production in the empire came from other emerging centers in the borderlands: the extractive industries of the Transcaucasus, particularly the oil production of Baku, and the manufacturing enterprises of the northwestern cities, most notably Riga and Vilna.

Riga provides an example of the rapid growth of industrial city islands in imperial Russia during the late nineteenth century, in a land that was still predominantly rural on the eve of the First World War. From 1867 to 1897, the population of Riga grew approximately 350 percent, from 77,468 to 288,943. A new industrial proletariat accounted for the largest part of the addition. In the same period, the urban population of the Russian empire grew almost twice as fast as that of the countryside. The population as a whole continued to grow as rapidly as it had for almost two centuries. By 1897, the Russian empire, including Finland, had a population of 128,967,198. Growth quickened somewhat in

[2] Goldsmith's figures. See Bibliography.

the late nineteenth century, when the decline in the mortality rate became more rapid than the rise in the birth rate. This was even more pronounced in the industrial cities. Nevertheless, the urban population of Russia amounted to only 9.94 percent of the total in 1863; 12.76 percent in 1897; and 13.2 percent in 1913. It was concentrated in a few big industrial cities and ports. Before the turn of the century, Moscow and St. Petersburg had passed the million mark, Odessa exceeded 400,000, and Kiev and Riga numbered over a quarter of a million. There were forty-four cities with a population of more than 50,000 by 1897.

In the 1890's, about one sixth of the population of the Russian empire was engaged in commercial and industrial, rather than in agricultural, military, and bureaucratic occupations. A much smaller percentage formed the industrial working force, and an even smaller number constituted a fixed, hereditary, urban industrial proletariat. The growth of Russia's factory working force during the period 1865–1914 can be seen in the following approximate figures (which include workers in manufacturing and metallurgical industries and in rail transport):

1865	706,000
1890	1,424,700
1900	2,373,400
1914	3,743,800

If approximations of the number of workers employed in water transport, government war plants, as well as the millions engaged in construction, are added to the 1914 figure, the size of Russia's industrial proletariat in the first months of the war would exceed six million (Khromov's estimate). However, even in 1914, a substantial portion of Russia's industrial workers were not what could be classified as a hereditary, urban proletariat, but were peasants working seasonally in the cities, or newly arrived recruits for year-round work in the factories, whose psychological and economic ties with the countryside were far from severed.

Only in the most highly mechanized industries, such as cotton printing and spinning, or machine construction, do we find second generation workers whose emotional and social world had become that of the city, the factory job, and the tenement. However, it has been estimated that by the turn of the century, half of Russia's industrial proletariat belonged to this group.

Working conditions during Russia's industrial revolution were as rigorous as those of the English industrial revolution of a century before. As in England, the coal miners suffered perhaps the greatest privations. The oil workers of Baku were exploited like colonial natives; and in central Russia, the lives of women and children were blighted in the textile factories by long working hours at low wages. In the late nineteenth century, the working day in most Russian factories exceeded twelve hours, as evidenced by legislation of 1897 that specified an eleven and one-half hour day. However, a decade later, the average work day in Moscow, Russia's most industrialized province, had been reduced to nine hours. This reflects the strength of the labor movement, which had gained impetus during the Revolution of 1905.

The growth of railroads was impressive. The period from 1859 to 1915—from the first year of really extensive railroad construction in Russia until the eve of the wartime crisis of this industry—saw the building of over 46,000 miles of track. By the end of the nineteenth century, almost 30,000 miles had been built, serviced by more than 3,000 passenger and freight stations, over 9,000 locomotives, and a rolling stock of several types, numbering 223,661 cars. By 1900, the number of full and part time employees approached one half million in an industry worth almost five billion rubles. Despite such a notable surge of growth, Russia's railroads still did not meet all the developmental needs of the country in the prewar years, although they were in a position to service most of the requirements of existing industry, and in some areas were overbuilt.

At the least, the necessary basis of rapid transit for the industrialization of a large geographical area such as European Russia had been created. Several main lines to carry grain from the agricultural regions to the Baltic and Black Sea ports had been put down. The big commercial and industrial centers of the interior had been linked by an extensive network of trunk and feeder lines. Ore, fuel deposits, and factories had been united to facilitate the growth of heavy industry. Passenger travel had been established on a regular basis between urban centers, as well as commuter services to the metropoli, most notably St. Petersburg. Subways for the capital cities were being discussed.

In the last years of the reign of Alexander III, the Russian government undertook the most ambitious railway project of modern times—the Trans-Siberian line. It took a quarter of a century to build; and by 1916, it was possible to go from Europe or Russia to Vladivostok entirely on rails. Such a vast and expensive project—a span of almost 4,000 miles, which cost over a quarter of a billion rubles—could only be justified on several urgent grounds. The eastern sections were built for military and imperialistic reasons, to facilitate the defense of Russia's east Asian fortresses and to penetrate China economically. The western sections were built primarily to develop Sibera—its imports and exports and its population. Millions of people could now migrate to the fertile southern parts of this vast region in a matter of days and weeks rather than years, and with an insignificant incidence of disease and mortality. The construction of the line was also designed to stimulate the development of Russian iron mills and machine factories.

The cost of building and maintaining railroads in Russia had always been exorbitant. Until the last few years before the First World War, they lost money, a cost absorbed by the state. Although the state had built and operated the first railroads, during most of the reigns of Alexander II and III it gave encouragement to private enterprise, foreign and domestic, to assume this burden. The government acquired most of the stock in the private companies and guaranteed a high rate of return. Direct state control of construction and operation, however, was found to be cheaper, and by the end of the century, policy had been reversed. From then on, the government bought and built most of the railroads. The railroads nevertheless remained a losing proposition, not only because of heavy indebtedness, but also because of rising costs, inefficient management, and the unstable political conditions of the first decade of the twentieth century.

On the positive side, there were productive efforts during the entire period of the railroad boom to modernize, consolidate, and rationalize the system. Operating expenses were trimmed, tariffs and exchange of cars were regularized, and new equipment was introduced. As in other Russian industries, as well as in the banks and insurance companies, extensive consolidation of both state and private operations took place. By the turn of the century, there remained only 31 large railways in the empire, 70 percent of them state controlled. Similarly, the railroad machine industry, which had been almost exclusively in the hands of foreigners in earlier generations, was by 1900 very largely controlled by Russians.

The growth of the railroads in the last half century of the tsarist period was not matched by a significant improvement of other means of transport. Few modern roads were built. By the early part of the First World War, highway construction, despite the added initiative of the zemstvos, barely exceeded by threefold the mileage of 1850, a mere 3,228 miles at the earlier date. The number of paved streets and roads was infinitesimal: a total of 266 miles, most of these in Poland. Rivers remained important arteries of domestic trade in the year 1900 as they had in 1500, despite the fact that many were frozen and unusable for a period extending far beyond the winter season, and in the summer were too shallow to be navigable for many types of vessels. Nevertheless, over 100 million tons of cargo, mostly wood, but also a substantial amount of grain, travelled Russia's rivers annually by the end of the nineteenth century. Little was done to modernize this system during the period of the railroad boom. The canal system that had been built in European Russia during the early 1800's was not expanded, and only one major canal, connecting the Ob and Yenesei rivers, was built in Siberia. Goods continued to be carried on various types of sail craft, barges, and a large number of rafts; by 1895, only 2,539 steamboats, or about one eighth the number of other more primitive types of vessels cruised Russia's 106,875 miles of navigable waterways. A Russian seagoing merchant marine was only feebly developed in the late tsarist period, despite some government aid. By 1900, less than 10 percent of the merchant ships entering Russian ports were Russian owned, and few of several hundred steamers had been built in Russia. Indeed, by 1914, over two thirds of Russia's small merchant fleet on the high seas were still wooden sailing vessels.

A small and vigorous communications system was created during the reigns of the last three tsars. By 1870, most of the cities of Russia had been connected by telegraph lines, including a five thousand mile link, the longest in the world, between Kazan and Vladivostok. By the turn of the century, Russia possessed almost 100,000 miles of telegraph lines. Tsarist statistics claimed a volume of messages which far exceeded the traffic of Western Union in the United States in the same year. At the same time, telephone networks had been built in most of the important cities of the Russian Empire, and a long distance line between St. Petersburg and Moscow had been established. The initial telephone construction had been undertaken by the American Bell Telephone Company among other private enterprises; during the 1890's and after, the Russian government assumed a dominant role in telephone development.

The development of manufacturing industries in the late nineteenth century displayed contrasts of growth and stagnation reminiscent of earlier periods of its development, as well as other areas of the post-Reform economy. From 1861 to 1913, the cotton industry grew at a rapid rate, and was substantially mechanized and concentrated. Russia became the world's fourth producer of cotton goods. As early as 1900, Russia's mills possessed over one third as many spindles as those in the United States; and most of her cotton fiber was grown within the empire, in Central Asia, rather than imported from the American South or the Middle East. Other areas of the Russian textile industry remained stagnant during the same period. The woolen industry, largely an estate industry in the days of serfdom, actually declined after the emancipation, except in the Kingdom of Poland. There was insignificant growth, both in woolen production and its technology by the end of the century. Russian peasants continued to produce vast quantities of linen in their cottages, although they also bought less, preferring garments made of cotton cloth. Moscow's tiny silk industry saw the founding of a few dozen new factories in the 1880's and 1890's.

The growth of Russia's metal working and machine manufacturing industries in the late nineteenth century, although substantial, was less spectacular than that of textiles. Large quantities of foreign machinery continued to be imported, which by 1900 amounted to about 25 percent of the total in use. The proportion for agriculture was much higher. From 1861 to 1897, the number of machine and metal working factories increased over six and one half times to a peak of 682. The number of workers in the same industries increased over tenfold, and production, by twice that proportion—evidence of the high degree of concentration. The machine industry was stimulated by the railroad construction of the last decades of the century. By 1900, 83 factories manufactured industrial and railroad equipment, employing over 125,000 workers, and selling a product worth 207,166,000 rubles in that year. Less than a sixteenth of this sum represented the total output of agricultural machinery, most of which came from small plants.

Heavy industry in late nineteenth-century Russia remained backward relative to consumer industry at home, and to heavy industry in other industrializing countries. Where the development was more substantial, the dependence on foreign capital and technology was great. The ancient iron industry of the Urals, technologically backward and heavily dependent on serf labor in the prereform period, declined in the period immediately following the emancipation, when many liberated factory serfs returned to the villages. Its growth in the industrial boom of the 1880's and 1890's remained slow. With the coming of railroads, the resources and location of the Ukraine made it much better suited for the development of an iron and steel industry, and most of the growth of these industries in the late nineteenth century took place in the southwest. By 1900, over half of Russia's iron and steel came from the Ukraine. The Russian steel industry, almost nonexistent before 1860, was producing well over 4.3 million tons annually by the beginning of the First World War. An essential ingredient in the success of the new Ukrainian metallurgical industry was not only government aid, but the application of foreign techniques, the importation of skilled labor and management, and the heavy investment of European capital. With all of this, and with increasing mechanization and a growing rate of productivity, Russia by 1900 was still producing only one fifth as much iron and steel as the United States.

Similarly, Russian coal production by the turn of the century represented only a small fraction of the output of either the United States or any of the major European coal producers. Although the industry expanded at a rapid pace during the last three decades of the old regime as a result of the needs of Russia's growing railroads and steel mills, one fifth of the domestic consumption on the eve of the Great War was satisfied by English and German supplies. It was the Don Basin, rich in both anthracite and bituminous coal, which saw the most spectacular growth of production before 1914. The older mines of the Urals and Moscow regions remained backward, and the immense reserves of Siberia feebly exploited. Almost half of the mines of the Don Basin, however, were controlled by foreigners. Technology was not very far advanced.

Like the coal of Siberia, the equally rich oil deposits of Baku were largely neglected until the 1890's. By that time, the several conditions essential for a rapid growth of the Russian oil industry had conjoined in the Caucasus. A market for fuel, lubricants, and kerosine had developed in Russia, but also, on a larger scale, in Europe and the Orient. Railroads and pipelines had been built to Baku; and a modernized oil extraction technology was being substituted for the primitive methods which had prevailed for decades. Finally, the giant oil combines of Europe and America had formed and were ready and eager to take over the Caucasian pools. The first oil boom brought production to almost twelve million tons by 1904, almost all from the Baku fields. The violence of the 1905 revolution in the Caucasus and competition at home and abroad caused a sharp decline of this hub of the Russian oil industry. A full recovery was never achieved during tsarist times.

The most backward of Russia's heavy industries until most recent times has been the chemical industry, which was negligible before the 1880's. Its main and very limited function prior to that time was the supply of some dyes to the textile industry. Railroads served both to bring down the costs of Russian chemical products and to consume such products themselves. Tariff protection facilitated expansion. Nevertheless, by the turn of the century, investment in the Russian chemical industry represented only 10.8 percent of the total capital of the six major heavy and light industries in the empire. A third of this capital was in foreign hands.

Of Russia's numerous agricultural and food industries, a final note should be taken of the industrial development of three during the last half century of the old regime. By 1914, Russia was a leading producer of tobacco products, superseded only by the substantial and progressive even in the period of serfdom, continued to enjoy strong government protection. The beet sugar industrialists, many of them wealthy landlords and bourgeois entrepreneurs from the Ukraine, had both the capital and the foresight to introduce extensive technical improvements in the refining process, if not in beet cultivation itself. As a result, beet sugar production jumped from just under two to about seventy-five million pounds from 1862–1863 to 1913–1914. However, the Russian product, with high costs of production and low crop yields, was expensive. Most of it was consumed at home, although some was exported to the Middle East. Russia was also a leading producer of tobacco products, superseded only by the United States and Cuba. By 1913, over 132,000 tons were produced in 235 relatively large factories. Inferior grades of tobacco, mainly the strain known as *makhorka*, were produced in large quantities for home consumption. A small amount of higher grades of tobacco was exported abroad. The manufacture of alcoholic beverages, a mainstay of the Russian economy and state finances since the eighteenth century, was expanded and facilities were modernized in the late nineteenth century, in part the result of a more enlightened tax system. Large distilleries replaced the small and primitive estate stills which had dominated the scene in most areas before the Great Reforms. In 1894, the government took over the liquor trade with the economic effect of increasing production, and the social consequence of intensifying alcoholism. The net revenue from the liquor monopoly rose over 50 percent from 1905 to 1913, to a total of 675 million rubles.

Despite a high rate of economic growth after 1885, despite the energetic fiscal and agrarian policies of the tsarist government, despite significant social change in the cities and in the countryside, Russia's industrialization by 1914 remained incomplete in many key sectors, and there was poverty and social instability among millions of peasants and urban dwellers. Russian capitalism had only begun to mature, and the dependence on foreign capital and technology was greater than ever. The puzzling and contradictory nature of Russian economic growth under the last three tsars was reflected in the writings of many economists of the time. The problem of industrialization was indeed the main theme of a famous debate that took place at the turn of the century between Marxists and agrarian socialist (narodnik) writers. Some narodnik economists questioned whether Russia was becoming a capitalist country; and others even doubted that the prevailing state policies and social forces would lead to full-scale industrialization. The Marxists, Lenin among them, researched diligently and argued forcefully against such propositions. The leading narodnik and Marxist scholars were, however, in agreement on several fundamental predictions: that Russia's industrialization would be unique from that of the West; that the peasant presented the most formidable stumbling block to Russian industrialization; and that the Russian state-to-be would play a significant role in promoting economic development.

These were, of course, wishes as much as they were prophecies. Despite the growing instability of the tsarist monarchy and bureaucracy and the alienation of the intelligentsia and industrial workers, Russia's fledgling capitalism was nonetheless vigorous and firmly rooted. The countryside was a social tinderbox, but was much more stable socially and productive economically in 1917 than it would be during the next two decades of atomized farming and violent reorganization. With the persistence of anachronisms and the rapid emergence of new forces, Russian society was coming apart at the seams, but it was far from being doomed. It took the most devastating war in Russian history to wreck this society and transform what had been only hopes into real possibilities.

3 / Industrial Disintegration, 1914-1929

The industrial history of Russia entered a new phase, not with the revolution of 1917, but with the outbreak of the First World War in 1914. As important as were the implications of the revolution for the industrialization of Russia, the war also changed the nature and direction of Russian industrial development for generations to come. The war set the stage for the revolution and for Soviet industrialization; the communist industrial system was built on the ruins of the Russian war economy. The war placed a strain on Russia's semi-industrialized economy which it could not sustain. This disruption was not the primary cause of the revolution, but the revolution and the prolonged civil war which followed it hastened the disintegration of Russian industry begun in the war. By 1921, Russia's industrial plant was producing at 13 percent of its prewar level: industrial production had been set back a third of a century, to just less than the output of 1885. The tendency toward nationalization and militarization of Russian industry began during the war and was greatly accelerated during the revolution and civil strife which ensued; it has continued ever since. The war meant the end of a consumer-based industry in Russia, until modifications in the direction of consumer goods production of the 1920's and most recent years. The war cut Russia away from the main markets of peacetime world trade, an isolation which endured until recent times. During the last part of the war, Russian agricultural production began to descend into the crisis and blight on the nation's economic growth from which it has yet to fully emerge.

The period from 1917 to 1921 is described by many historians, employing official designations, as "War Communism." The succeeding eight years of peacetime industrial recovery is similarly termed the "New Economic Policy," or NEP. War Communism in Russian industry, apart from its ideological significance, meant in many respects previous wartime policies with stricter state control, more comprehensive labor mobilization, and more drastic coercive measures. Following this, the period of recovery from invasion and civil war was slow, and Soviet industry functioned essentially on the basis of the tsarist plant until the late 1920's. The new, peacetime economy resembled in some fundamentals the pre-1914 state-patronized capitalist one, but did not represent so much a retreat from socialism as a rebuilding of Russia's shattered industry on the basis of small-scale farming. Drastic changes, amounting to a new phase of Russian industrialization, did not come until 1929. The period from 1914 to 1929 thus represents a kind of interim in the industrial history of Russia—a Time of Troubles (recalling the historical designation for the early years of the seventeenth century), of destruction, and stagnation. So disastrous were the effects of war, revolution, and civil strife that the industrialization process was not only halted, but for a while reversed. Lack of reform of the economic anarchy created in the countryside by the revolution brought Russian industry to a crisis in the late 1920's.

RUSSIAN INDUSTRY IN WORLD WAR I

The outbreak of hostilities in the summer of 1914 caused a jolting, although temporary, disruption of Russian industry. There was an immediate and sharp curtailment of markets, supplies, and manpower. By the end of the year, however, the empire's factories had converted from a peacetime footing, and some key war industries were flourishing. Big profits were to be had. This boom continued for the first year of fighting. It was an unnatural development. Although many industries essential to the war effort prospered, those producing noncritical goods suffered a depression which deepened as the war went on. In the first thirty months of the war, almost twice as many industries were shut down as were opened. By 1916, prolonged shortages of fuel, food, raw materials, and the lack of manpower, machinery, and adequate transport were causing a more serious dislocation of all Russian industry. By the winter of 1916–1917, industry was producing at about three-fourths of its prewar level.

Military operations caused no direct damage to Russian industry of any serious dimensions. Cities were not shelled extensively, nor were factories destroyed on any large scale by artillery, aerial bombings, or fires, as in the Second World War. German conquest of the industrial regions of Poland caused shortages of coal and diminished the supply of textiles, resulting in higher prices for these goods. However, although such losses of territory, manpower, railroads, and industries were substantial, they did not crucially affect the productivity of the remaining majority of factories in the unconquered provinces of the empire.

A much more serious catastrophe befell Russian industry as a result of the almost total strangulation of foreign trade. This began immediately in 1914 and lasted for seven pinched years. Declaration of war with the Central powers shriveled the value of Russian exports by over a third, although most of the foodstuffs previously sold to Germany were needed to feed the wartime armed and labor forces. The result was a passive balance of trade which grew to massive proportions as Russian imports more than doubled from the 1913 level. This deficit of billions contributed greatly to the inflation of the ruble in international exchange. More ominous for Russian industry, however, was the effect of enemy military occupations and naval blockades. The main western gates of Russia were closed to commerce. Equipment and supplies vital for Russian industry could be brought in only through undeveloped, obscure, and distant ports, such as

Murmansk in the north and Vladivostok and Nikolayevsk on the Pacific. Russian railroads had not been built sufficiently to service adequately these peripheral ports. This resulted in crucial shortages in fuel, raw materials, and machinery, and the resultant forced inactivity of many Russian factories. Production, particularly of iron, fell drastically.

The Russian transportation system was incapable of bearing the burdens of modern war, and was itself disrupted by war conditions. Russia was called upon to mobilize troops and deliver supplies on a scale far exceeding the scope of the continuing civilian tasks of her railways. At the same time, the small railroad machine industry almost immediately converted to war production. Locomotives, cars, and replacement parts were not easily come by in the conditions of virtual total blockade under which Russia suffered. The result was a breakdown of overstrained equipment which by 1917 assumed the proportions of a disaster. The transportation system began to creak to a halt. Not only were Russian industry and the war effort seriously threatened, but the disruption of transport itself was accelerated when fuel no longer reached the locomotives. By the eve of the Russian revolution, the railway system was operating at less than half its peacetime capacity, while at the same time being called upon to assume a burden over ten times in excess of its prewar tasks. Russian industry, progressively cut off from stocks of fuel and materials that gathered dust in railroad yards and sidings, suffered no sharper blow from the war. The river and canal fleets of Russia also deteriorated, although not as markedly or with such severe consequences.

Even before the war took its toll, the industrial labor force in Russia was small and unproductive by comparison with many European countries. No more than six million men—less than 4 percent of the population—were employed in industry, construction, and transport when the war began. Many of these workers were actually peasants by origin, outlook, and the persistence of legal and familial ties with the village. Some were seasonal workers. The instability of this marginal proletariat later became manifest in its rapid disintegration and return to the countryside, particularly after the 1917 revolution, when starvation began to stalk the cities.

By the early part of that year, over fifteen million Russian men had been taken into the armed forces, of which approximately 20 percent by reason of death or disability would never return to their peacetime jobs. The decline in population growth resulting from war conditions accounted for double this number. This amounted to a labor force of nine million, permanently lost to the Russian economy. Although two thirds of the total number of men conscripted were peasants, this meant that the much smaller contingent taken from the factories could not be replaced by exhausted village reserves. The labor shortage was partially alleviated by the employment of prisoners of war, refugees, Chinese and Korean coolies, and ultimately and in largest numbers, Russian women. Children down to the age of twelve also were recruited. The number of male workers employed in Russian industry dropped by about 20 percent during the first two years of the war. The inexperienced replacement labor was far less productive, but it was also cheaper. The result, according to Lyashchenko, was the coexistence of hundreds of thousands of unemployed workers with labor shortages, production setbacks, and higher wages. Nevertheless, real wages, even in war industries, began to decline with inflation. Peacetime industries, where wages had always been low among seasonal peasant workers, suffered even more.

The decline in real wages was the primary cause of numerous strikes. The continuing and intensifying process of the concentration of Russian industry during the war set the stage for larger work stoppages. Political factors, however, played an important role in many labor disturbances. By early 1917, most strikes were so motivated. Workers continued to be faced by economic problems, but had come to realize (or were persuaded by revolutionary agitators) that only the government could solve the food and other painful shortages caused by the war. However, the government's answer to strikes was to draft the protesting workers—not an innovation in Russian state tradition, hardly popular, and only stimulative of new unrest. By 1916, after an initial show of patriotic support for the regime by Russia's workers, the abnormally high prewar level of strikes very nearly had been reached. Approximately a quarter of the industrial working force went out in that year, in larger groups and for longer average periods of time per striker. About 2,100,000 work days were lost. This constituted a very small loss to Russian industrial productivity in view of the increased working hours imposed by the war effort. Nevertheless, it was indicative of growing discontent and a spirit of rebelliousness on the part of the Russian worker, which were to have serious consequences for industrial management and production during the revolutionary period.

The war also pushed the peasant into characteristic forms of rebellion. The traditional resort to rioting in the villages, mutinies, and desertions from the army were soon to come, but before this, he turned naturally to a passive and much more ominous form of obstruction which was to plague the economy and threaten the leadership of three regimes for years to come: he cut back on the delivery of his produce. The backwardness of Russian industry, and the further curtailment of industrial production resulting from the war, particularly in areas important to the peasant consumer, were the primary causes for reduced agricultural output. This made itself felt almost immediately in the cities, which experienced food shortages. Over the coming years the long-range effects of starving cities and vanishing grain surpluses would be a drying up of sources of industrial expansion and a disintegration of the industrial proletariat. The breakdown of the railway system and the mobilization of horses for the war contributed to food shortages, but the main cause of declining agricultural production and sales was the collapse of the Russian consumer industry and the curtailment of consumer imports and of farm machinery. Prices for manufactured goods rose to the point where it was no longer worthwhile for the peasant to exchange his grain for inflated rubles. The "scissors crisis"—the disparity between lower grain prices and higher prices of consumer commodities, which was to plague the soviet regime in the 1920's—first made its appearance in June, 1915. It intensified in 1916, although there was some relief during the first months of the Revolution when grain prices rose. To meet the crisis, there were unsuccessful experiments with rationing and price fixing. The storehouses of the cities continued to empty. On the eve of the revolution, in which "bread!" was the opening cry, the government planned but never had the opportunity to implement a program of compulsory deliveries. However, such a drastic measure was soon to become a foundation of Soviet agrarian policy.

Russian state finances on the eve of the war were healthy enough to enable the government to weather the first months of hostilities without abnormal pressure on the treasury. The currency—for seventeen years on a convertible gold standard—was stable; the 1913 budget showed a comfortable balance of about 15 percent of the total revenue (3,417,000,000 rubles); foreign borrowing had not been resorted to since 1910; and the national debt since that year had diminished by about 2.5 percent, to 8,811,000,000 rubles.

As war costs skyrocketed, ordinary revenues plunged. At the beginning of hostilities, the average daily cost of the war was 8,000,000 rubles; by the beginning of 1916, this sum had quadrupled. Revenues declined with the curtailment of foreign trade and domestic consumption, but this loss was minimal. The one staggering blow from which the tsarist budget never really recovered was the elimination of the biggest source of state revenue at the very beginning of the war. Prohibition of alcohol consumption was declared, thereby diminishing state income by over 25 percent. This was not a move to conserve grain, but a temperance measure, although it did not stem the drunkenness of the many who poisoned themselves with moonshine. However, some improvement in the health of factory workers was noted and attributed to the government's ill-timed experiment in temperance. The fiscal result in the face of massive military expenditure was a menacing deficit, which was never fully met by domestic and foreign loans, although these totalled 25,000,000,000 rubles by the time of the 1917 revolution. As in previous wartime crises the government resorted to the printing press for supplementary resources. The ensuing inflation reduced the paper ruble to a third of its prewar value by the beginning of 1917.

Even less successful than its effort to finance the war was the attempt of the Russian government to organize an industrial base for the extensive and exhausting military operations in which the country was quickly and totally absorbed. The tsarist bureaucracy soon proved to be incapable of performing such a complex task. A war mobilization of industry nevertheless took place, through the initiative of business management in coopera-tion with the Duma, the zemstvos and other semiofficial organizations. While the zemstvo and town unions consolidated on a national level (Zemgor) to facilitate the war effort and supply of the army, businessmen formed into numerous local "War Industries Committees," with a central body in Petrograd. These committees in turn cooperated, not always free from sus-picion and rivalry, with other groups founded and granted sig-nificant powers by the Duma. Such agencies asserted increasing control over industries crucial to the war effort, particularly those involved in metallurgy, textiles, and fuel.

In this way, Russian industry was converted almost exclu-sively to war production to fulfill state orders, while consumer industry and the private market contracted rapidly. At the same time, the burgeoning militarized sector of the economy was sub-jected to a much more rigorous state control of prices and dis-tribution. The coal and leather industries became in effect state monopolies. In other industries, centralized state agencies tightly controlled the market. By the end of 1916, a degree of state control of industry unprecedented in Russian history had been attained. However, private property in industry had not been abolished; and the government remained dependent on the experience and organizational skills of business management, as succeeding regimes would for at least another decade. Neverthe-less, the state control and militarization of Russian industry, for the next half-century to remain among its primary characteristics, definitely had begun.

Although producing at about three fourths of its prewar capacity, Russian industry by February, 1917, was far from a state of collapse. More serious industrial disintegration was to come after the February Revolution, but still Russia would go on. Russian industries, of course, were hurt seriously by the war, particularly consumer industries. On the other hand, some industries prospered and grew from 1914 to 1917. However, the most significant aspect of the industrial history of Russia during the First World War as this relates to the Russian revolution is not that there was an industrial decline, but that Russian industry was insufficiently developed to sustain the burdens of modern large-scale military conflict. This resulted in a transportation breakdown, shortages of consumer goods, fuel, and food, inflation, and a lowering of the standard of living. All of these calamities helped to stimulate the discontent, demoralization, and anarchy with which the tsarist regime, already fatally weakened by institutional, political, and personal evils, was unable to cope. Almost overnight, it collapsed, in February, 1917.

The Provisional Government, although clearly more representative of private industrial interests than the monarchy, was nevertheless, a fledgling regime with weak and inexperienced leadership, its authority seriously challenged by a number of powerful, organized, and more popular opposition groups. It was less capable than the tsarist autocracy of checking the rapidly spreading disorganization of industrial production and the disintegration of discipline among factory workers, to say nothing of being up to mobilizing the economy for the renewed war effort which it undertook. Inflation, already a serious threat in tsarist days, became rampant under the Provisional Government, although the total collapse of the Russian currency was yet to come. The Provisional Government's attempt to introduce a direct taxation program in the midst of a mounting fiscal crisis failed, as did its war bond drives and efforts to borrow from abroad. The entrance of the United States into the war at this time did not result in any substantial or sufficient infusion of aid to her new ally. Inevitably, the Provisional Government resorted even more than its predecessor to the traditional expedient of printing-press money, with the result that, by August of 1917, the ruble was worth less than half of its value only a few months before, on the eve of the February Revolution. The overall wartime inflation of the ruble now approximated 600 percent.

The Provisional Government reasserted the tsarist policy of industrial mobilization by state control with the cooperation of management, labor, and public organizations. Most of the monopolies over key industries that had been developing under the wartime aegis of the old regime were continued. Agricultural policy focused on the same targets, but was somewhat less conservative. Tsarist state lands were nationalized, and a state grain monopoly was established, restricting the sale of grain to the government, fixing its prices, and providing for the seizure of all grain unlawfully withheld by the peasantry. To coordinate this program a "Council on Questions Relating to the Development of Productive Forces of the Country" was established in May, 1917. This was later reorganized as the Economic Council and the Central Economic Committee, the former body including not only representatives of the government, business, and the zemstvos, but also spokesmen for the trade unions and the soviets.

Despite these overtures to the public the Provisional Government lacked the authority to implement to any significant degree its ambitious economic programs, nor could it stem the mounting rebelliousness on the part of businessmen, workers, and peasants alike. Such activity was drastically curtailing agricultural and industrial production. Industrialists refused to cooperate with the labor program forwarded by the Government and by the soviet, while responding to labor unrest with lockouts. Workers began to seize factories and expel managerial personnel. The peasantry rioted and withheld grain in resistance to government procurement policy. They deserted in droves from the army to hasten back to their villages. The result of numerous work stoppages and obstructions was a decline of production in industry and in the coal mines that was greater than ever before. War production in some areas was almost at a standstill. The railroads fell into serious disrepair, operating at only a small fraction of their former capacity. Belated aid from the United States in an effort to keep them running was of no avail. Food supplies for the cities dwindled to an all-time low, in the face of the most rigorous rationing impositions. As early as the middle of May, 1917, the Minister of Trade and Industry, Konovalov, warned: "We must openly and honestly recognize that under the old regime, this catastrophe was never outlined so clearly and vividly as it is outlined now . . . a catastrophe which is ready to shatter to its foundations and to annihilate our entire economic life. . . ." By October of 1917, the economic situation in Russia had become even more hopeless. The triumphant Bolshevik revolutionaries of that month were the heirs far more than they were the makers of an industrial shambles, the further crumbling of which they were unable to stop for some years.

THE BOLSHEVIK REVOLUTION AND WAR COMMUNISM

"As meagre and colorless as a routine police report," said Trotsky of the October Revolution in Petrograd. "The bourgeois classes had expected barricades, flaming conflagrations, looting, rivers of blood. In reality, a silence reigned more terrible than all the thunders of the world. The social ground shifted noiselessly like a revolving stage, bringing forward the popular masses, carrying away to limbo the rulers of yesterday." Trotsky's dramatic and romantic image of the anticlimactic and notably bloodless events which carried the Bolsheviks to power in Russia obscures the very real and significant economic consequences of the October Revolution. True, the revolutionary insurrection itself—limited in space, time, and the number of active participants—had almost no immediate disruptive effect on Russian industry. The factories, like the theaters and cabarets, continued to function normally while more momentous political changes were taking place. Whether the Revolution brought forth the "popular masses," as Trotsky claimed, is not essential here; it did place in control of the Russian economy and Russian industries a new group, whose purposes, ideas, experience, and political position differed quite radically from those of the former rulers. This represented the greatest significance of the October Revolution for Russian industrial development in the coming few years. Generally speaking, the views, training, and methods of the new leaders of Russia were often more a liability than an asset in the complex task of developing, to say nothing of managing, Russian industry.

Marxist theory presented no great barrier to the Bolsheviks in their formulation of economic policy. Lenin had developed a highly voluntaristic version of Marxism, which extolled the vigor and creativity of human action over the determining power of external forces or logical consistency. Although rigidly dogmatic in the matter of revolutionary power, Lenin was quite willing to adjust theory to expediency at almost any point in order to advance and preserve that power. There were opposing points of view (which later inspired political factions) among his followers—people who tended to be more doctrinaire and radical in economic matters. However, the bickering caused by these dissenters over issues of economic and industrial policy was never much more than an annoyance, which Lenin, with dictatorial power and tremendous personal prestige, easily overcame.

The most serious deficiency of Marxist-Leninist theory as applied to Russian industrialization was not its dogmatism but the fact that no comprehensive and practical program for the economic management and development of the country had been developed by Marx or his Bolshevik apostles prior to the Revolution. "Nothing has been written about this yet in Bolshevik textbooks," Lenin was to say in 1918 in reference to these problems, "and there is nothing in Menshevik textbooks either." For decades, the main concern of the Bolsheviks had been the gaining of power, not the use of it. Sophisticated intellectuals, amply endowed with scholarly and literary talents, had produced a huge fund of polemical literature, elaborate tactical programs, and probing critiques of the existing society, but little of this cerebral energy had been diverted to the task of planning its replacement. Few of the Bolshevik leaders on the morrow of the October Revolution had extensive, utilizable experience in practical economic matters beyond the field of engineering. They were masters at the art of organizing workers for disruptive purposes, but knew nothing of the management of industry. State finances were a mystery to them; and the peasant was a formless and fearful spectre in the distant countryside, whose problems were alien to the liberators of the urban proletariat.

Probably the Bolsheviks' greatest asset for running the Russian industrial economy was that in some ways they were politically a much stronger breed of men than their predecessors. Resourceful, energetic, tough, and determined, they waded boldly into seemingly impossible tasks, and were not scrupulous about the use of coercive measures in the realm of economic policy. Decisions which imposed hardships on large numbers of people were made without flinching. Nor were the Bolsheviks hesitant, particularly when their situation was desperate, to use violence in the implementation of economic policy, especially against those classes comprising the overwhelming majority of Russian society whom they considered their class enemies—most peasants and all of the "bourgeoisie." However, this free resort to force proved in the long run to be a great economic liability because it provoked die-hard and massive resistance to their policies. By temperament and by training, the Bolsheviks were ready to deal with overt political and military opposition. It was passive economic resistance, in the form of slowdowns in industrial and agricultural production, sabotage, mismanagement, and apathy, which they were often unable to cope with.

Moreover, to achieve their revolutionary aims, the Bolsheviks had encouraged and stimulated widespread anarchist and syndicalist tendencies, particularly among Russian factory workers. Now they were faced with the task of controlling this whirlwind, of restoring the industrial discipline they had helped to disintegrate with such success. Although large numbers of workers, soldiers, and peasants were unwilling to oppose the Bolsheviks, or were actively supporting them, the illegitimacy of the Bolsheviks' power and the violent way which they chose to achieve and maintain it inevitably provoked armed resistance from many segments of Russian society beyond the old ruling classes. The Bolshevik Revolution, almost from the beginning, brought on a long, bloody, and costly civil war. Like the war with Germany preceding it, the civil war had a blighting effect on Russian industry. The same militant and aggressive Bolshevik policy which provoked war within Russia very nearly delivered the death blow to Russian industry when the tsarist foreign debt was repudiated and foreign assets and industries were confiscated. Such acts made soviet Russia an international pariah, isolating Russian industry from the world economic community in terms of trade, investment, and credit. If the chains of imperialism had been cut, the lifelines to sustain a starved and moribund economy were now completely severed.

The period from the October Revolution to the spring of 1921, encompassing the Civil War between the Bolsheviks and their domestic and foreign enemies, witnessed a regression of the soviet economy into conditions which in some respects could be termed primitive, and which recalled tsarist times of generations before. Industrial production by the end of the Civil War had been drastically curtailed, to about one fifth of what it had been in 1917, and to 13 percent of the 1913 level. Heavy industry had almost ceased to function; the iron industry, for example, was producing at about 2 percent of the prewar output. Although more than this was being produced in other sectors, no Russian industries of significance could put out even half of what they had been capable a decade before. As a result of territorial losses in the Civil War and the Brest-Litovsk peace settlement with Germany, Russia had lost the largest part of entire industries— sugar, iron, steel, and gold the most prominent among them. Almost half of her industrial workers were gone. The last important trade arteries had been severed by White armies. On top of this, the Allies had imposed a commercial blockade from 1918 to 1920. This had effectively destroyed any vestiges of foreign trade not already stifled by the Germans during the World War, leaving cities and factories in Muscovite isolation, deprived of any substantial source for the replenishment of machinery and parts. The part of Russian industry still able to operate was itself reduced to the function it had first served under Peter the Great: the production of armaments under state contract. Consumer industry disappeared.

The Russian railway transport system, already seriously strained by three years of war with Germany, was brought to the point of collapse during the three more years of civil conflict that followed. War and blockade were the main factors contributing to the disruption of the railroad system, although anarchical labor conditions also played a role. Not only did the armed forces commandeer half of the nation's locomotives during the Civil War, but, since fighting took place along or near the railroads that supplied the battlefields, the same armies were responsible for much destruction of railway equipment and track. Most of the equipment, however, simply wore out and became unrepairable because of the lack of replacement parts. Between the Revolution and the fall of 1920, over 10,000 locomotives were put out of commission. Less than a third of Russia's prewar locomotive force was still operative by that time. Several thousand railway bridges had been destroyed or were unusable, as were hundreds of miles of track. Some track construction did continue during the Civil War, although the construction of new railway equipment dropped to almost nothing by the end. By that time, Russia's territory had been reduced to the proportions of old Muscovy, and the near destruction of her modern transportation system meant a regression to communications conditions of the previous century.

An even more pronounced sign of the regression of the Russian industrial economy during the Civil War was the "disintegration of the proletariat," as it was called by Bolshevik leaders at the time. Destruction wreaked by military operations, territorial losses, evacuations of civilians, the breakdown of transport and distribution, and the depletion of food supplies in the cities —all played a part in a wholesale urban disintegration. There was a flight of factory workers and city dwellers to the villages, where they could at least cultivate the land and eat. By 1921, the Russian industrial working class numbered less than half of what it had been in 1913. The population of Russian cities had declined drastically, in some cases by a third. Indeed, with critical fuel shortages, the cities were disintegrating physically. By 1920, about a fourth of the wood frame houses of Petrograd had been picked to pieces for firewood.

Money was also disappearing, as rampant inflation brought currency to the point of worthlessness. Banks were closed and state budgets ceased to function. While the Russian economy reverted to barter, a black market of vast proportions arose. As the result of losses of the most fertile areas of the old empire, as well as of labor power and equipment, and of the pilferings of black marketeers and speculators, but most of all because of the concealment of food hoards in the villages and the refusal of the peasants to grow crops for government requisition, a famine, largely of human invention, descended on Russia's cities. Agricultural production during the Civil War fell to less than half of its prewar level. As early as the spring of 1918, Moscow factory workers were living on a few ounces of bread a day. Many intellectuals, the most dispensable and least able to fend for themselves in such primitive conditions, starved to death.

The most significant economic development of the Civil War period came in the countryside. Russia's agricultural system reverted to the primitive past, as the large estates as well as many kulak plots were rapidly dismantled, and almost all farming reverted to tiny holdings of less than ten acres. This was one of the most devastating, spontaneous, overnight social revolutions of human history. The ominous result of this fragmentation of land tenure was that Russian agriculture, so organized, could no longer sustain full-scale industrial growth. The crisis in industry would take several years to mature, while the agrarian problem in the Civil War was an immediate one—starvation or survival.

So it happened that by 1921, the Russian industrial economy was in ruins. The Bolsheviks, as well as those inside and outside of Russia who refused to accept their insurrectionary claim to authority, were responsible for this wreckage. These conditions were the price of war and revolution. The Bolsheviks, who had no alternative short of surrender, which was as repulsive to them as to their enemies, accepted this cost. Although for a long time believing their cause to be lost, they nevertheless attempted to remedy an almost hopeless economic situation. In such a plight, the policies which they instituted during the period, and which they called "War Communism," were not part of a long-range plan dictated by socialist ideals and designed to create a socialist society. They were essentially expedients employed to meet the desperate conditions produced by the military operations of the Civil War and the intervention of the European and American powers, by the foreign blockade of Russia, by the resistance of the peasantry and workers to state mobilization, and finally, by the Bolsheviks' own lack of experience in state finances and industrial management. This did not prevent such expedients from being construed by idealists, wishful thinkers, or propagandists as socialist experiments, rather than stopgap remedies by embattled socialists. The illusion that Russia was moving forward into socialism could be conjured to hide the harsh reality of a disintegrating economy.

Nowhere were these illusions more cherished than in the realm of banking and currency. The Bolsheviks, admittedly illiterate in such matters, were at the same time strangely attracted to the construction of instant financial utopias, more than for any other area of the new economy. Initially, the banks were seized because of the need for funds and the obstinate refusal of the bankers to cooperate with the revolutionary regime. These harshly pragmatic acts were followed by two years of aimless, idealistic experimentation, which ended in the abolition of the existing credit institutions in the belief that the time had come to introduce higher forms of socialist financial administration. Similarly, currency, inflated to worthlessness, was extolled as a weapon for destroying bourgeois power, while schemes were advanced to create the moneyless utopia of socialism.

Of the less visionary institutions improvised under War Communism, the most significant for Russian industry was the Supreme Council of the National Economy (*Vesenkha*), whose establishment was decreed in December, 1917. *Vesenkha* was given vast powers. It was subordinate only to the Council of People's Commissars, although Lenin tended to view it as something of *Sovnarkom*'s economic equivalent. *Vesenkha* never attained such a paramount position, but its control of Russian industry was almost total from the beginning. On the one hand, it was empowered to plan and coordinate industrial development, and on the other, to confiscate, reorganize, and run all industries. All state economic agencies were placed under its roof. Thus, it became the heir to the central economic administrations of the Provisional and tsarist governments at the same time that it was nationalizing the industries, banks, and other business enterprises of Russia. By 1920, 60 percent of Russia's industry had been effectively appropriated by the Bolshevik regime. The running of this vast industrial empire soon became *Vesenkha's* primary and absorbing function; planning was entrusted to yet other agencies.

Vesenkha grew into a mammoth bureaucracy. The wartime agencies of the tsarist and Provisional governments which had been created to coordinate production and distribution for entire industries were transformed into centralized administrations for these industries, known usually by the abbreviation *glavki*. The *glavki*, of which there were about seventy by 1920, were given virtual control over most of the important industries of Russia. They worked independently of the provincial and local Councils of National Economy (*Sovnarkomy* and *Gubsovnarkomy*), which regulated smaller enterprises and were concerned with a broad range of local economic problems. Thus, we find created a *Glavneft* for the entire oil industry, *Glavavto* for all automobile manufacture, *Tsentrosakhar* for sugar, and so on. Such centralization might easily place hundreds of enterprises and hundreds of thousands of workers in one huge bureaucratic satrapy. The *glavki* were run by boards consisting in many cases of the old factory managers and technicians, but including a preponderance of trade union members, workers' representatives, and party officials. In turn, the *glavki* appointed similarly composed boards, as well as directors and inspectors for local plants.

The creation of *Vesenkha* and the *glavki* was an attempt to solve the problem of wartime industrial supply by superbureaucratization and centralization. Tight controls certainly were necessary in such an anarchic period, but they were applied with such a vengeance under War Communism that the result was persisting bottlenecks and a serious misallotment of resources. It was simply impossible in the conditions of the Civil War for one central agency to control hundreds of dispersed factories, large and small, or even to be cognizant of their essential needs. The doors of many plants closed for lack of fuel or supplies which a central board, swamped in bookkeeping and inadequate or inaccurate statistics, had not been able to allocate. As bottlenecks multiplied, a priority system was developed for industries essential to the war effort. However, such reallocations only bled other industries, and ultimately furthered the strangulation of the whole system.

The idea of managing boards composed of workers, communists, businessmen, and technicians, although laudibly democratic in character, did not function efficiently and soon was replaced, particularly on the lower echelons, by the time-honored principle, both tsarist and Bolshevik, of one-man bureaucratic authority. Moreover, the *glavki* system demanded a sophistication and discipline of personnel which was not to be found in revolutionary Russia. The workers included on managerial staffs might obey orders coming from a communist hierarchy, but they were without administrative experience. The old timers—business executives, engineers, and civil servants drawn into the new system more out of a cynical sense of self-preservation than material expectation or political conviction—could hardly be called upon for inspired administration by the regime that had dispossessed them.

Vesenkha and the *glavki* thus do not represent initial measures aimed at creating a rationally organized socialist industrial system, but rather an overbureaucratized control of Russia's factories called into being by the dire exigencies of the Civil War. However, the idea of a master plan by which to marshal all of the nation's resources for long-range industrial growth had appealed from the very beginning to Lenin, Trotsky, and many of the Bolshevik leadership. They had not been overly impressed by the tsarist tradition of state mobilization of the people with all its inefficiency, although Lenin, like Stalin, maintained a grudging admiration for Peter the Great. The efforts of the wartime imperial administration and the Provisional Government to coordinate the industrial economy under centralized agencies provided some experimental precedents and guidelines, but nothing more. Marxist writings indicated that the planning and amalgamation already achieved by capitalist industry was the right road to socialist industrial organization, but provided no specific prescriptions. Such designs, however, were outlined by planners in the imperial German government during the First World War, whose work Lenin greatly admired and openly proclaimed as the model for communist Russia. He was also impressed by the proposals for a long-range plan forwarded by a Russian monarchist engineer, Grinevetsky.

Implementation was another story; the costs and chaos of the Civil War prevented anything more than talk, which was plentiful and cheap, about the big plans of the future. Although at its inception *Vesenkha* was given the powers to become Russia's central planning agency, these powers were never used and were quickly set aside. With the end of the Civil War in sight by 1920, planning was taken more seriously. Numerous proposals advocating comprehensive economic plans to be formulated by super planning agencies were advanced. Trotsky emphasized overall coordination of soviet economic development by a supreme planning council; Lenin was attracted to more specific and immediately realizable projects. The first Bolshevik "plan" —not purely a paper utopia, but a program which the government attempted to finance and implement in some way—was the plan identified with GOELRO (State Commission for the Electrification of Russia), established in 1920. GOELRO, with a staff of hundreds of economists and engineers, was not merely an electrification program, but a coordinated plan for the rapid economic development of soviet Russia. Newly built hydroelectric stations would provide power for additional railroads and machine factories, which in turn would mechanize Russian industry and agriculture. The growth of heavy and consumer industries was to be promoted, for the former more than the latter, over a period of ten to fifteen years, at the end of which industrial production would be at 150 to 200 percent of the 1913 level. Such a plan was to be put in motion with an initial investment of seventeen billion rubles.

Although more concrete in some respects than other schemes afoot at the time, GOELRO was still a projection rather than a program, as witnessed by the fact that construction on the first hydroelectric station envisaged by the plan was not begun until 1922. GOELRO was significant only as evidence that the idea of a master plan to rapidly further the industrialization of Russia and to manage an economy totally controlled by the state had become fixed in the thinking of the Bolshevik leadership.

From its earliest days, the Bolshevik regime was faced with an industrial labor shortage, the result of desperate economic conditions of the Civil War, but also of its own unrealistic policies and of anarchistic forces released by the revolution. Hundreds of thousands of workers fled starvation in the cities. Others seized factories in what was called "workers' control" (a tendency encouraged by the Bolsheviks just prior to the October Revolution), but which actually represented at best a spontaneous kind of syndicalism, and at worst, pillaging of plant stock for consumption or sale. In a situation where discipline was rapidly disintegrating and wages might not be forthcoming, those who continued to show up for work were little motivated, when not blatantly incompetent to deal with the problems of factory management. "Expropriated" or uncooperative owners and foremen were no longer available to keep the factories going. Experimentation with wage equalization, never carried beyond symbolic gestures, such as obliging party and state officials to take a cut in salary, did little to improve industrial morale.

The soviet government was faced with two extremely urgent labor tasks: recruiting more industrial workers and increasing the productivity of those at hand. At the beginning, Bolshevik labor policy was a curious mixture—like other Bolshevik policies during "War Communism"—of expediency and a gloss of utopianism. In the end, the regime resorted to coercion and to the Russian tradition of state impressment and militarization of the labor force. Immediate steps were taken as a matter of necessity to restore morale, discipline, and state control in the factories. Wage incentives and bonuses in money or kind were instituted—when the currency had not become almost worthless or supplies dangerously scarce. Attempts were made to utilize revolutionary and patriotic enthusiasm through the designation of special units of "shock" workers, who were encouraged to deliver higher quotas. "Communist Saturdays" were introduced and publicized, as a way of gaining an extra day of voluntary, unpaid labor.

When popular support of these experiments was not forthcoming, the government began to transform them into obligations. Ultimately, compulsion became the only way of assuring, if not a high level of productivity, at least the minimal supply of labor. As in the days of the tsars, a general corvée was imposed on the population. The main utilization of this forced labor was for public works. Internal passports were reintroduced to insure fulfillment of work quotas and to restrict flight. Soldiers were ordered to mines and factories, while workers were placed under military discipline. Political prisoners in the concentration camps were put to forced labor. Lenin was reverting to the methods of Peter the Great, as he declared at the time that he would not hesitate to do.

The customary wartime expedients of rationing and price-fixing proved insufficient to cope with growing food shortages. The rapidly depreciating currency was unacceptable to the peasants as exchange for grain. Few industrial products were available for barter after the needs of the army had been met; and those goods which could be scrounged for shipment to the countryside proved inadequate to buy the vast bulk of produce needed to quell the hunger pangs of the cities. The few thousand collective farms promoted by the state were quickly shown to be a depressing failure. As early as May, 1918, the government turned in desperation to a policy of grain confiscation. Lenin called for "iron detachments of the conscious proletariat"—armed units of workers and communists of proven zeal—to do the job. These *prodotryadi* (produce detachments), as they were known, duly marched out to the villages to sequester grain at gunpoint. In the villages, Committees of the Poor (*kombedy*) were set up to perform the same task, for which they would receive a liberal cut of the confiscated goods. The objects of the campaign were the kulaks, the village rich, the rural "bourgeoisie." The word "kulak" (literally: tight-fisted), as later under Stalin, often came to mean any accused peasant who did not cough up, although in

1919, again presaging the big collectivization drive a decade later, there was an easing of pressure on the numerous *serednyaki,* the "middle" peasants.

The policy of produce confiscation could be interpreted (as it was presented in official proclamations) as class warfare between the rich and the poor, the kulaks versus workers and peasants. What the kulaks frequently saw were not workers and peasants carrying revolution to them, but uniformed troops and officers pointing firearms at them. They responded to such harsh measures, imposed for almost three years, with various kinds of resistance. In the fall they hid their grain from the *prodotryady,* and in the spring, ceased to cultivate beyond their own needs. As a last resort by 1920, they began to rebel on a large scale in the provinces. Some even raised the banner of mutiny within the armed forces. The Bolsheviks knew how to deal quickly with hoarding and rebellion, as they proved on the bloodied ice of Kronstadt and against the Tambov peasant uprisings. The passive resistance of underproduction was something with which they were unable to cope; it provoked the food crisis which brought an end to War Communism and the development of fundamentally new lines of policy in agriculture and industry.

INDUSTRIAL RECONSTRUCTION AND CRISIS
UNDER THE NEP

The New Economic Policy (NEP) was a series of measures introduced in 1921 and 1922 during a period of rebellion and famine. Like the preceding War Communism, it was not a new policy in the sense of creating socialist forms of organization in industry and agriculture, or of promoting comprehensive and rapid industrial growth. In the primitive and desperate conditions to which the Civil War had reduced Russia, issues of ideology and modernization could only be subordinate to the more fundamental ones of survival and power. NEP, as Lenin himself insisted, was basically a political decision, rather than an economic one; the foremost question in the minds of the Bolshevik leaders in 1921, as it had been for three agonizing years, was how to preserve their power. In terms of immediate, emergency measures, this meant averting the impending food crisis in the cities; in the long run, it meant rebuilding the Russian industrial economy. The only way that these two essential objectives could be achieved was by ending the crushing and arbitrary system of taxation of the peasantry. A guarantee that the peasant owned a portion of what he could grow, above and beyond the very grim level of marginal subsistence that had been his lot during the Civil War, would revive in him the incentive to produce crops for the market. The cities would buy these crops, thus alleviating critical food shortages and urban discontent. At the same time, the sale of produce and relief from onerous requisitions would increase peasant income and provide a market for industrial goods. Peasant purchases would stimulate the recovery of Russian industry.

There was no other policy available to the Bolshevik regime, given the domestic and international circumstances of the time. Communist revolution had failed to materialize in any of the major industrial nations of the West. This deprived soviet Russia of the food supplies, military and technical aid, and capital funds which might have enabled the Bolsheviks to sustain themselves against a hostile and uncooperative peasantry, while rebuilding the shattered economy and even implementing a program of modernization. They were alone in a hostile capitalist world; their leadership was on the verge of several years of paralyzing factional struggle; and they had barely begun to build the military and police institutions and bureaucratic apparatus which would have enabled them to heavily tax the peasants and at the same time force them to produce for revenue. Such a policy would have involved the rapid construction of an immense system of state administered rural slavery. It is doubtful that Lenin, although not averse to rigorous measures against grain hoarding, ever contemplated building such a system; all the evidence would indicate that his policy toward the peasants by the end of 1920 had become one of realistic accommodation. Lenin's acute sense of realism, sharpened by the spectre of peasant revolt, led him to appreciate the impossibility of a policy of mass coercion in the countryside at the end of the Civil War, just as it obliged him to brand as dreams and sentimentalism the socialistic agrarian programs forwarded by left wing idealists in the Bolshevik party at that time.

It is obvious that the New Economic Policy was concerned primarily with agriculture rather than industry. Industrial growth was subordinated to agricultural recovery and was made dependent on it, although several dramatic master plans and targets were created on paper in the offices of *Gosplan*, the new state planning agency. However, these castles in the air, like the grandiose electrification programs of War Communism, did not have the secure and necessary economic foundations of a program of industrialization. They were propped by the far less sustaining base of a makeshift policy of petty commercial recovery from the primitive natural economy that the Civil War had created in the countryside. To the degree that the rural economy became commercialized through increased peasant production, sales, and income, Russian industry would revive. Such industry would not be socialist in nature, but essentially a form of petty capitalism. However, the decision to permit millions of peasants to sell part of their produce necessitated the creation of a capitalist economic structure which extended far beyond the limits of the Russian village and led ultimately to a reorganization of Russian industry.

The first step in this process and the cornerstone of the New Economic Policy was the decree of March 21, 1921, and subsequent decrees of the same year, which replaced the *prodrazverstka* (produce requisition) of War Communism with the *prodnalog* (income tax). These decrees specified that the new tax should not exceed half of the former requisition, although in practice, the rates for the most important agricultural products in 1921 and 1922, such as grain, potatoes, and eggs, were slightly higher than 50 percent. Nevertheless, the new decrees signified the end of arbitrary confiscation; the peasant now paid a fixed tax, and owned at least half of what he produced beyond what was required for seed and personal subsistence. Anything more that he wished to grow was his own personal property.

The *prodnalog* was a tax in kind; money had long before ceased to exist in soviet Russia. It was hoped at the beginning that the government could facilitate some kind of direct exchange between the villages and cities through special transport arrangements, thereby preventing the growth of trade in free markets and the re-creation of a system of petty commercial capitalism. However, no resources were available to finance what would have been a very elaborate system of distribution. Nor could the government prevent the peasant from undertaking to sell his own produce to buyers who offered him the best return, any more than it could curtail the huge black market which had been engaging in such transactions during the Civil War. Inevitably, the peasant's right to buy and sell, to transport goods to market, and to possess money were affirmed. These rights were soon extended to workers, cooperatives, and factories. Local markets, bazaars, fairs, and retail stores were rehabilitated. The peasant who was allowed to act as his own merchant in the rural marketplace soon stood at one end of a rapidly expanding economic system that eventually culminated in large-scale commercial enterprise in the cities, controlled by capitalist middlemen of old and new vintages.

One concession led to another in a spontaneous growth of essentially capitalist relationships, which the state had sponsored, but which it could not contain without disrupting the economic recovery which it so desperately sought. From commerce, the new practices extended to property, labor relations, state finances, and industry. If the peasant was to be encouraged to cultivate more land, he required more security than simply the right to own and dispose of some of the fruits of his labor. Consequently, his rights to hold and use land for the foreseeable future and to hire labor were confirmed in legislation of 1922.

The more the peasant brought to market, the greater the demand for money. The growth of a money economy in turn increased the need for credit. Beginning in 1922, state banks for the financing of commercial enterprise, industry, and public works (Vneshtorgbank, Prombank, and Elektrobank, among others) were established. A network of credit institutions was developed in the countryside. Property insurance was revived.

The demand for money also made imperative a currency stabilization. This called for measures to balance the state budget, and first on the list was an increase in tax revenues. Money taxes of various kinds were added to the *prodnalog*. A vodka monopoly, similar to the tsarist one, was restored, among numerous other indirect taxes. A kind of poll tax, the "general civil tax," was introduced in 1922, although this was consolidated with the other direct levies in the following year. The sale of government bonds domestically, also begun in 1922, provided a significant additional source of revenue.

The first soviet ruble—notes of several issues, known collectively as the *Sovznak*—literally worthless at the end of the Civil War, was replaced by the *chervonetz*, which was partially backed by gold and was equal to about five American dollars. The revitalization of Russia's foreign trade helped to build up gold reserves. By 1924, confidence had been restored in soviet money, and its stability and circulation had developed to the point where a transformation of the *prodnalog* into a money tax was possible.

The agrarian, trade, and fiscal programs of the NEP forced a reorganization of Russian industry. Growth of free markets in the countryside quickly revived the cottage and petty factory industry which could supply these markets with manufactured goods. The rights of this industry were in due course protected. Large-scale industry also was obliged to buy and sell in the growing commercial economy, and was soon permitted to do so by the government. Moreover, it became clear that if the government were to balance its expenditures with its new revenues, it could no longer bear the excessive costs of financing and operating Russia's larger industries. These costs could be reduced in several ways. The policies elected were not the only alternatives; labor, for example, could have been put under compulsion and taxed more heavily, as in the Civil War and later under Stalin. In 1921, the soviet government followed the path of least resistance, a characteristic option of the NEP. Thus, it made sense to think in terms of the state's relinquishing the burden of maintaining industry through various kinds of leases. These could be granted to private entrepreneurs of Russian origin, especially the experienced former owners of plants and factories, or to newly formed cooperative organizations, stock companies, and foreign industrial firms. Additional funds could be saved by the reorganization of those industries which the government wished to retain under more direct tutelage. However, for a business concern to be more efficient, to cost less, and to adjust to the newly developed market economy, it was necessary here, as in other areas of soviet state policy, to relax controls and to allow increasing independence of local and individual action.

The smallest industrial enterprises, beyond the very large number which had never been nationalized at all, were leased by the thousands, many to former owners. An equal number were taken over by cooperatives. Most of these "enterprises" were small shops, or even family and individual manufacturing operations, producing for the peasant market. Their growth was a natural response to the free rein permitted them by the government and to the agricultural recovery under free market conditions. Indeed, these private enterprises may be considered essentially a part of the NEP agricultural renewal, for they produced only a small fraction of the total industrial product and employed less than 5 percent of industry's labor force. Private ownership of larger forms of industry, however, did not prove to be any more significant. Agreements made with foreign firms, beginning in 1921, accounted for less than 1 percent of the total number of industrial enterprises, workers, and value of production after more than six years. Privately financed industrial stock corporations were similarly insignificant.

The largest part of the Russian industrial economy under the NEP remained under more direct state control, although with considerable decentralization and debureaucratization. This is what the leadership proclaimed as its socialist "commanding heights." The government continued to run the banks and railroads and to conduct all foreign trade. Large-scale industry, however, was completely reorganized. The *glavki*—the cumbersome, centralized industrial bureaucracies of War Communism —were vastly reduced in number. The larger of the enterprises which had been administered by the *glavki* were reorganized into hundreds of "trusts" (*tryesty*). The trusts were groupings of factories into central or local networks of varying size within the same or allied industries. Although their land and physical plant were formally owned by the state, and they remained nominally under the jurisdiction of *Vesenkha* and its remaining *glavki*, the trusts were virtually independent of state control and inspection. Operated essentially like capitalist enterprises—such procedures were given a new, less offensive designation, "economic accountability" (*khozrashchot*)—their main obligation was to make profits. Nevertheless, a substantial part of these profits went to workers in the form of welfare funds and to the state to amortize loans.

Such, in briefest outline, was the New Economic Policy as it related to Russian industrialization. The question of how "new" the NEP was was seriously debated at the time. Fears and hopes were sounded throughout the world, mainly by apprehensive socialists and dispossessed capitalists, about the "restoration of capitalism" in Russia. Although some of the former small-scale industrialists were allowed to lease what had been their property, while the property rights of peasants were tacitly affirmed, and a few bankers and capitalists of the old regime attained positions of influence in the soviet administration, this hardly amounted to a return to capitalism. Quasi-legal guarantees and bureaucratic posts could be swept away by the same stroke of the pen that had created them, in the personal and arbitrary autocratic system that Lenin had developed by 1921. The state maintained a fairly rigorous control over all the key sectors of the industrial economy. There was no organized or armed opposition which could seriously challenge its power after the guns of the Civil War had been silenced.

If the NEP did not restore capitalism, neither did it resurrect much else of the Russian economic past. Many features of the state-patronized industrial system of the tsars may be said to have reappeared under the NEP, most notably the tsarist industrial plant itself. This had been restored on the basis of prewar technology, for there were no resources available for the gigantic task of replacing, expanding, and modernizing Russian industry. The degree of state control over soviet industry was vastly greater than what had been developed by 1913 or even 1917. Moreover, the extensive foreign investment in Russian industry and commerce, which had amounted to a virtual control over large sections of the economy in tsarist times, had come to an abrupt end. Soviet industry had become both independent and isolated, although not self-sufficient, particularly in matters of technology. The political changes which had taken place in Russia after 1917 had no immediate effect on her technological backwardness.

The biggest break with the tsarist past was in agriculture. It can be argued that the real Russian revolution in the social sense was not the expulsion of the landlords, industrialists, tsarist generals, and Liberal politicians in the Civil War, but the vast agrarian upheaval provoked by the collapse of authority and by Bolshevik slogans, in which most of the remaining estates (and much of the kulak land as well) disintegrated into more than twenty-four million tiny subsistence farms. Whether this was a "bourgeois" and not a "socialist" revolution, or simply a storm of anarchy which no one could control, can also be debated. It is indisputable, however, that the peasant land seizures of this violent era so changed Russia's economic structure that previously conceived programs for the country's industrial development—tsarist or socialist—no longer applied. The NEP was not, and could not have been, either a restoration of the old state-patronized capitalist system devised by the tsar's ministers of finance or the building of socialist industrial institutions. It was instead, a pragmatic adaptation to the new agrarian conditions. The NEP was essentially a policy of agricultural and industrial recovery, and almost certainly the only policy that would have averted the economic and political collapse of Soviet Russia. However, the same policy which provided the only means for the recovery of rural Russia proved to be inimical to industrial growth. Russian industry was helped to recover from the ravages of war, but once this recovery was achieved, the NEP became essentially a system perpetuating industrial stagnation. Unsuitable for the promotion of substantial economic growth, the NEP policies also were ineffective in the face of a series of crises which disrupted the economy as a whole. Nor were they designed to reform the underlying conditions which produced these crises.

The fundamental problem of the NEP period was the inability of small-scale agriculture producing for an open market to sustain the rapid industrialization required to complete the development left unfinished in tsarist times, particularly in the sphere of heavy industry. The backwardness of soviet industry was first revealed in the crisis of 1923, popularly and officially known as the "scissors crisis." [1] The scissors crisis was not one of low agricultural production and procurement generally, as in the war or in 1921, nor was it a question of declining production of commercial crops as in the late 1920's. In 1923, the Russian countryside, relative to other areas of the economy, overproduced. The weakness was that of Russian industry, which failed to show adequate growth after more than two years of the NEP. Rural industry and handicrafts made a quick comeback with the growth of the peasant market, but heavy industry improved feebly from its almost total collapse in the Civil War. It remained a budgetary millstone for the government, draining off just over 15 percent of total expenditures in 1923. Consumer industry, profiting from its extensive decentralization, made some strides toward recovery, but by 1923, was producing at less than half of its prewar level. Costs were high, wages were low, and industrial unemployment had reached mass proportions.

Agriculture, on the other hand, had experienced a much more rapid recovery, although commercial crop production was still far below the prewar level. Nevertheless, after a devastating famine in the lower Volga region during 1921, in which twenty-

[1] So named because lines on graphs of comparative agricultural and industrial prices during the fall of 1923 took the shape of an opening pair of scissors.

five million people starved, the crops of 1922 and 1923 proved to be excellent. As a result, agricultural prices began to fall. By the end of the year, they had dropped to half the level both of 1913 and of a few months before. Industrial prices, dictated by the backwardness of many industries and the monopolistic distribution practices permitted them under the NEP, had almost doubled in the same period. No longer able to buy, the peasant curtailed his production, while the industrial trusts, financially well off as the recent recipients of liberally dispersed government bank credits, refused to sell their products for what the market demanded. Thus, both the agricultural and the industrial sectors of the economy were receding into a crisis, as the gap between the prices for their respective products widened. The government was able to close the scissors in 1924 by forcing price controls on the trusts, by exporting grain, by alleviating the peasant tax burden, and in the last resort, by using police forces to crush the industrial unrest that deteriorating wages and currency fluctuations had provoked. It could not, however, solve the more basic problems of inflation, unemployment, industrial inefficiency, and underproduction without a comprehensive program of industrialization, and this was possible only if the production of marketable agricultural goods was vastly increased.

Although the scissors, albeit under control, continued to haunt the soviet economy after 1924, a far more serious crisis first became apparent in 1926. The crisis of 1923 had been one of recovery; the new dilemma was one of growth. In 1923, the revival of agriculture had far outstripped that of industry, producing a recession on both fronts. By 1926, Russian industry had very nearly attained its prewar capacity, but agricultural production began to decline. Industry had reached a point where it demanded investment for expansion and modernization, while the agricultural sector was becoming less and less capable of providing the resources which could be shifted for this purpose. This was not merely a matter of allocation of priorities by the government, although the issue was hotly debated at the time by the Bolshevik leadership (see Chapter 4). By 1928, the problem of agricultural underproductivity had become one of life or death, involving not only the fate of Russian industrialization, but, as in 1921, hunger in the cities, and the survival of the regime itself.

The year 1926 marked not only the beginning of the crisis which would bring an end to the NEP, but also a turning point in soviet industrial history. It was clear by the ninth year of Bolshevik rule that industry had substantially recovered from its breakdown in the Civil War. Signs were also accumulating to indicate that the same industry, which had utilized for its restoration essentially the plant and equipment built a generation before under the tsars, was becoming obsolete. It was wearing out. Expansion and modernization would shortly become the necessary and urgent alternatives to stagnation or even breakdown. It was not entirely coincidental that the fourteenth congress of the Communist Party of the Soviet Union, meeting in the winter of 1925–1926, for the first time resolved to give some priority to industrialization, although no substantial action was taken for some time.

It was also in 1926 that an ominous decline in Russian agriculture first set in. Although overall production was nearing the prewar level in that year, commercial crops, which had only attained about 84 percent of the output of tsarist times, began to dwindle. As we have seen, the main reason for this discrepancy was the disappearance in the revolution of the large estates and farms which had produced almost all of Russia's cash and export crops. A few estates had been preserved and operated as state farms, but these proved to be a failure. The *serednyaki* and *bednyaki* (middle and poor peasants) on millions of tiny subsistence farms now ate (and drank) almost all of Russia's annual agricultural product. The growing population of the cities alone required more than a third of what the state was able to procure each year. With such procurements declining, it would only be a matter of two or three more years until the government would not only be unable to export any grain, but would have to import it to feed the cities. The grain shortages, dangerous in themselves, came at a time when the government was obliged to increase the tempo of industrialization. This would require, not just the previous feeble attainments of commercial agriculture, but vastly larger grain procurements.

The kulaks, who fell from grace and came under increasing attack after 1925, were blamed by many for the crisis. Actually, most of Russia's poorer peasants, who produced 80 percent of the market crop, were equally "guilty" of hoarding produce from the state requisitioning agents. The government itself was also seriously to blame for the crisis because it had failed to develop policies fostering technical improvement, land consolidation, and voluntary collectivization among the poor, and because it had followed an erratic price policy, which was probably politically motivated.

By 1928, the New Economic Policy was descending into a crisis—a dead end, as it has been described. The escape of an industrial revival no longer seemed possible, only a stagnation into economic dependence on the West that would spell the end of the impoverished and corroded peasant dictatorship created by the Bolsheviks in the name of socialism. Russia did escape from this dead end and at the same time began one of the most massive industrialization drives in modern times. The way out was not determined solely by economic calculations and expediency, as in the 1921 crisis. There were crucial political—and personal—factors at work, for if the soviet economy had not substantially altered since 1921, vast political changes had taken place.

4 / The Second
Industrialization Drive,
1929-1953

The second industrialization drive in Russia—an economic change very different in its objectives and methods and far more comprehensive in its scope than the earlier industrial growth under the last tsars—may be pinpointed as beginning on November 7, 1929. It was on this day, hardly more than a week after the stock market crash which signalled the Great Depression in the United States, that Stalin made public his order for a total collectivization of the Russian peasants at breakneck pace. The two events and the economic developments which ensued upon each are not related, but they may be likened and contrasted. Both involved the suffering and privation of millions of people. However, one marked the beginning of an industrial depression; the other set in motion an industrial revolution—although not without its own very serious setbacks.

The immediate economic background of Stalin's industrialization drive can be seen in the changes in the soviet economy and soviet economic policy in 1928 and 1929. Agricultural production and procurement, in a process of decline during the late 1920's, reached the danger point in 1928. As pressure for food and saleable produce mounted, the government resorted increasingly to coercive procurement measures. The NEP was regressing into the *prodrazverstka* of Civil War days. At the same time, its industrial system was abandoned. In the spring of 1929, the First Five Year Plan was launched. This only intensified the agricultural crisis to the point where the industrialization effort was threatened with collapse.

As important as these economic changes were in bringing about the revolution of the plan era, there were political developments during the 1920's which also formed a necessary basis for the Stalinist industrialization drive. Ideological and scholarly trends were also decisive; during these years, debates took place among soviet economists, party leaders, and contenders for power. These debates are of great interest to the student of economic thought, and have been recognized by economists as one of the earliest sophisticated attempts at development theory. The issues which were raised are essential for an understanding of subsequent state policies in soviet Russia.

THE RISE OF STALIN AND
THE SOVIET INDUSTRIALIZATION DEBATES

The most significant political event of the late 1920's in Russia was Stalin's consolidation of immense dictatorial power. This was of crucial consequence for the future industrialization drive, because such a total economic effort and stern discipline of the nation would have been impossible without a high degree of concentration of the coercive and propagandistic instruments of government. The history of Stalin's rise to leadership in soviet Russia has been detailed in many biographies and political histories. It will suffice for the purposes of this essay to emphasize that by 1928, Stalin had already forged a powerful machine for totalitarian industrialization. The Communist Party of the Soviet Union, the highly disciplined and centralized organization that Lenin had built during two decades of conspiracy, revolution, and civil war, had passed into Stalin's grip. He had eliminated all major rivals in its higher echelons. He controlled its agencies of surveillance and conducted its purges. He had built both a party and a state apparatus loyal to his person, as well as a large and militant force of party stalwarts in the countryside.

Although the intelligentsia remained relatively unrestrained and the army had developed an independent professional *esprit*, the powerful political police forces were ready to do Stalin's bidding. The harnessing of the intellectuals and the officers corps was soon to come.

To understand the industrial revolution of the Stalin period, one must have some appreciation of the mind and character of the man who possessed such vast power. There can be no doubt that the industrialization of soviet Russia would have been very different without Stalin or a man of similar objectives and qualities; but there were few among the communist leadership of the 1920's of both the ruthlessness and the stature of Stalin. Although many followed his standard—a large cadre of tough, young *apparatchiki* without whom the implementation of his policies would have been difficult if not impossible—many others, particularly those of the older revolutionary generation who balked at his methods, were killed on his orders.

It would be as simplistic to put at Stalin's door all of the crimes, exploitation, and mistakes that were involved in the industrialization drive of the 1930's, as it would be naive to attribute to him all of Russia's victories and achievements, as was done by the Stalin cult. However, it is incontestable that Stalin did make the big decisions, and it is probable that advisors and favorites exerted very little real influence on him. The fact that his policies worked and accomplished great things does not refute the proposition that there were politically possible, economically viable, and morally more humanitarian alternatives. Nor is a purely economic explanation of what happened tenable, if it assumes that the major decisions, since they achieved success, were made on the basis of a rational calculation of necessities. Decisions also reflect the character of the people who make them as well as the political pressures to which they are subject. Soviet political life by 1929 had produced a certain kind of leadership which tended to behave in certain ways. Stalin stood at the pinnacle, and largely controlled a powerful bureaucratic apparatus, which had its own morality and certain political interests which determined its behavior. Whether this machine was the inevitable product of tsarist tradition, of the revolutionary movement and mentality, or of the anarchy and violence of wartime and revolutionary Russia can be debated. Stalin, it is clear, was both the product of these times, and the creator and master of the political machine which set out to industrialize soviet Russia in a more brutal way than had hitherto been contemplated by any of the communist leadership. Stalin did not use force to industrialize Russia because it was necessary; Stalin used force because he was Stalin. His role in both the industrial achievements of soviet Russia and the method of industrialization was great; the process cannot be understood without knowing the man.

Stalin was a very intelligent man, sometimes brilliant in his capacity to grasp complex issues with lightning rapidity (as in the realm of foreign affairs). Nevertheless, he was by all evidence a poor, indeed an indifferent, economist. Throughout his career, he had undergone very little training and had gained only meagre experience in economic matters. Stalin was what may be termed a voluntarist in economic policy making: the determinism, and respect for human and natural capacities of the professional economist, were alien to him. Trained in the school of Lenin, he believed that the human will could triumph over most obstacles. Stalin tended not to heed advice contrary to his determinations, and to view such disagreement not merely as misjudgment, but as cowardice or treason. Such an attitude, enforced by a rigorous punitive system, resulted in his being told very largely what he wanted to hear. The consequences of this system of fear and flattery in the realm of industrial policy were sometimes costly blunders.

Stalin was ruthless. There is no truer characterization of Stalin's cruel willingness to sacrifice his peasantry to the cause of industrialization than that of Milovan Djilas, the wartime observer of the Russian dictator: "He was one of those rare and terrible dogmatists capable of destroying nine tenths of the human race to 'make happy' the remaining tenth." Stalin's obvious hatred of the peasants is not as easy to explain as his anti-Semitism and other prejudices, since he himself was of peasant origin.

However, his indifference to wholesale peasant suffering was no doubt strengthened by years of struggle against the obstinate rural masses, and reinforced by Marxist theories of class warfare between city and countryside.

Stalin was not afraid of the peasants. He was a fearless and a stubborn man, and a gambler. Once committed, he was not one to quit or compromise, but rather, was reinforced in a determination to push all the way. The bigger and more grandiose a project, the more unattainable a goal, the more it seemed to appeal to Stalin. From monster eight-engined airplanes and mammoth self-glorifying statuary, to massive hydroelectrical projects, "giant" wheat farms, and fantastic schemes to change the Russian climate, the despot's romanticism of bigness was to be of great economic consequence for Russia. In 1929, it was the idea of mass collectivization at breakneck speed that mesmerized Stalin.

Although he later made a fetish of planning, Stalin did not proceed at the beginning from some original or elaborate blueprint for the industrialization of Russia. His economic position was inconsistent in the 1920's, and the most important of his economic ideas were appropriated from his political opponents of that time. When he had eliminated all opposition, he began to apply these ideas. However, Stalin's character imbued the implementation with elements of extremism and violence which had not been envisaged by the originators. Nevertheless, to understand his program, one must first look into the discussions that took place among soviet leaders and their economic advisors in the half-decade prior to the industrialization drive.

The industrialization debates were one aspect of a deep cleavage among soviet leaders, which involved not only economic analysis, but also the political intrigues of the time, and beyond that, basic views of revolution and of human nature. The schism between the "Right" and the "Left" (as it was known then) seems to be a more or less permanent division of socialist movements, dating back to the late nineteenth century and expressing itself over basic issues, even today. After the Russian revolution, the Right position in economic matters represented the official policy of the soviet government from 1921 to 1929–the NEP. When the NEP was finally and fully discarded, those who continued to expound this position were branded as "oppositionists" or "deviationists," until they were purged by Stalin.

The foremost spokesman for the Right was Nikolai Ivanovich Bukharin. Bukharin argued that a continuation of the NEP with certain modifications would bring about the completion of Russian industrialization and would create socialism. This would unfold in a very gradual process. It would be wasteful adventurism to push revolutions abroad, since capitalism had undergone a revival. Its collapse was not imminent. Hence, aid for the industrialization of soviet Russia could not be expected from friendly socialist regimes, although capital might be obtained by granting concessions to foreign businessmen and by exporting grain. However, the mainspring of industrialization was to be found within Russia; an industrialized socialist state would have to be and could be built in one country. This was to be achieved by increasing agricultural production. As the Russian peasant became more productive and wealthier, there would be more grain for export and more food for feeding the growing cities. More raw materials would flow to the factories. The rural market for industrial products would expand, and increased savings would accumulate in the countryside, which would provide funds for industrial investment. As industry expanded, costs and prices would diminish and the market would grow. Such a cooperation between city and country, worker and peasant, as Lenin had taught, was essential to the economic well-being of Russia. By the same means, Russian industry would be able to expand gradually beyond the renovated tsarist plant when this had reached its capacity. Although this program encouraged a class of capitalists in the rural as well as the urban areas (*kulaki, chastniki*), it would eventually achieve socialism. Socialism would result because the soviet state would retain control of the "commanding heights" of urban industry, and because voluntary collective farms—with the advantages of state support and the virtues of higher production—would attract the poorer peasant and check the power of the kulak. However, the peasants, particularly the more productive ones, had to be won over to socialism; to revolutionize them by expropriations, heavy taxes, and other forms of exploitation would only provoke resistance in the form of decreased production. This would both defeat the purpose of industrialization and pose a threat to the regime.

The Rightist program for industrialization was challenged almost at its inception. By the end of 1923, a formal protest had been presented by forty-six high-ranking party members, and debate continued for several years. Although the "Left Opposition," as it was known, grouped itself around the figure of Trotsky, the foremost exponent of its economic ideas and its program for industrialization was the economist Yevgeny Preobrazhensky. Ultimately, it was an extreme version of the Left program that Stalin adopted and implemented. Even at the beginning, the Left program was a far more radical one than that of the Right. The Left advocated revolution outside of Russia, revolution against the peasants within the Soviet Union, and an industrial revolution. The latter meant not simply an expansion of the existing consumer industry, but a total overhaul of the industrial system which would emphasize the construction of heavy industry, technology, the development of the transportation system, and the harnessing of new sources of power.

Where was the capital to be obtained for such a gigantic economic effort? Soviet Russia had no colonies to plunder; and there were no wealthy and friendly socialist states to provide aid (although the Left was more optimistic on the score of international revolution than the Right). Without the colonies or foreign investment that had provided the capitalist countries with funds for their "original accumulation" of capital for industry, Russia would have to turn within herself and finance industrialization with a different type of "primitive socialist accumulation." The existing industrial capital had been seized by the Bolsheviks at the very beginning of their rule. Sufficient funds had been available to repair the wartime destruction visited on this plant, but by the late 1920's, the tsarist plant was not only reaching its prewar levels and capacities, but it was clearly beginning to wear out. Eventually, its returns would diminish, unless there was very large investment to modernize and expand Russia's entire industrial system.

The source for such an investment in a politically outcast, primarily agricultural country such as Russia, argued the Left, was the countryside. The government would have to turn against the peasants who would be forced to provide the funds for industrial investment, the food and raw materials for the cities, and the grain for export. This sacrifice would be made by a "pumping" (*perekachka*) of the peasants by means of taxes, price adjustments, and requisitions. As Preobrazhensky summarized it: "To express the problem in the most easily understood words—can the burden of developing state industry and reconstructing its whole technical base be borne on the shoulders of our three million workers alone, or must our twenty-two million peasant householders take a share in this too? The experience of our existence during the seven years of the revolution has answered this question and continues to answer it in the affirmative."

For several years, the Right and Left factions argued the economic, political, and ideological correctness of their respective positions. The Rightist policy, it was charged, would bring on industrial stagnation, and would invigorate capitalism in Russia, which would constitute a political threat to the regime. Far worse, the Rightists retorted, the Left policy of crash industrialization and arms race would disrupt the economy more rapidly and devastatingly through disproportionate development, peasant resistance, and agricultural underproduction. These would be the inevitable result of exploitative measures applied by the state in the countryside, measures which resembled more the tsarist system than the building of socialism.

During the industrialization debates, which were accompanied by factional struggles, Stalin changed his position, moving from the Right to the Left. At the same time, he developed a third alternative. Essentially, Stalin's program for the industrialization of Russia combined the most realistic proposals of the Right and Left, and replaced their more utopian and humanitarian elements with bureaucratic and violent solutions. It is difficult to determine when Stalin conceived of his alternatives. It is probable that they were not blueprinted at any one time, but were reached over a period of several years in the course of his struggle for power. The grain crisis which threatenened the regime once he had achieved this power, and after the party had sanctioned an industrial crash program, was very probably a turning point in his thinking. In such pressing circumstances, Stalin did not hesitate to choose the more drastic alternatives to coerce a recalcitrant peasantry. That he grossly underestimated the resistance that his agrarian and industrial policies would provoke seems evident. Almost always, this resistance was met with force. Rarely did Stalin retreat; but he did back down when there was no other way.

As early as 1925, Stalin championed the idea first advanced by the leaders of the Right that it was utopian to posit the survival of the soviet regime on communist revolutions abroad. Socialism and industry could and had to be built in one country. However, it was not until after three more years of contradictory and non-committal statements, which kept essentially within the framework of the NEP, that he began to clarify his position, by the winter of 1927–1928. From the discredited Left faction, Stalin now appropriated the idea that only a rapid and comprehensive industrialization would prevent economic stagnation and provide a substantial base for soviet power. At the same time, he also accepted and expanded on the conviction of the Leftists that a "tribute" (*dan'* to use his own words) would have to be extracted from the Russian peasantry to provide the capital for such a major effort. By the summer of 1928, he had fully converted to the Left agrarian policy of "pumping" the peasantry. Sometime during the winter of 1928 or spring of 1929, Stalin hardened this policy into one of purge.

This may be seen as Stalin's own contribution to the Left industrialization program—the idea that by the use of massive state power peasant resistance to taxation could be overcome and the requisite quotas of grain delivered. He apparently believed by the fall of 1929 that he had accumulated adequate power to overcome resistance to such a reduction of the countryside. He had eliminated his major rivals from among the old Bolshevik revolutionary leadership, and had built up a massive bureaucratic machine in the party, police, and state which most recently had been extended with the dispatch of thousands of tough and desperate *apparatchiki* out into the rural areas. There remained only the details of technology, organization, and procurement, and the maturation of a crisis which would permit the invocation of state power for rigorous measures against the peasantry, or any other opposition to government policy. In the matter of technology, organization, and procurement, Stalin found his panaceas in the Machine Tractor Stations (MTS), collectivization, and the *kontraktsiya* ("contract," a collection system which was later discarded). Whether there was a real political crisis in Russia in 1929 can be debated. There is no question, however, that in the spring of that year, Stalin, in his speeches, began to conjure the spectre, however insubstantial, of a gigantic capitalist threat—a plot, which linked kulaks, NEPmen, bourgeois wreckers from the old regime who had wormed their way into the soviet establishment, and foreign saboteurs. This plot could only be dealt with by criminal prosecution. A trial of such traitors had in fact already been staged (the Shakhty trial of 1928).

An unquestionably genuine economic crisis developed in 1929. It was in the spring of that year that the first comprehensive program for industrial development, which became known as the First Five Year Plan, was put into operation. Although in most other respects a crash program, the First Five Year Plan envisaged not a forced, quick collectivization of farming, but a very gradual transformation. In half a decade, 80 percent of Russia's farms would still be individually controlled. The party leaders, Stalin among them, believed that agricultural raw materials, food, and cash crops sufficient to sustain a major industrialization program could be produced by the joint efforts of an expanded state sector and a rigorously controlled private domain of agriculture. The wealthier and more productive kulaks and serednyaks would be obliged to market over half of the necessary quota. But even greater hopes were placed in the several million acres of large-scale state farms (*sovkhozy*), which had been formed out of prerevolutionary estate land not seized by local peasants. Soviet leaders, and particularly Stalin, also looked optimistically at the growing number of voluntary collective farms (*kolkhozy*), formed mainly by the poorer peasants. The combined production of the state and collective farms, it was predicted, would approach that of the private sector, or at least reduce the government's dependence on what individual peasant entrepreneurs chose to market.

These hopes were not realized during 1929, which became a year of crisis and violence. Agricultural production as a whole declined, and for a while government procurements dropped severely. At the same time, the First Five Year Plan moved into full swing. Not only was the industrialization program threatened with collapse in less than a year unless something was done to increase procurements, but the cities faced food shortages, rationing, and the consequent breakdown of discipline and morale. The government turned increasingly to force as a means of extracting produce from a recalcitrant peasantry. Procurement campaigns were launched. An army of zealous tax collectors imposed the crudest of pressures and penalties on those peasants who refused to deliver grain. Some peasants resisted with violence—they rioted, started fires, shot officials—but most were frightened into acquiescence. Procurements increased, finally jumping to a much higher yield than in the previous year. At the same time, the pace of collectivization was successfully accelerated, although at nothing like the speed of what was to come. Thus, as Russia's economic crisis deepened in the fall of 1929, the use of force as a productive method of resolving this crisis also increased. It was this atmosphere of violence and breakdown that provided the background—although not necessarily the primary cause—of Stalin's next major decision.

THE STALINIST METHOD OF INDUSTRIALIZATION

Toward the end of 1929, after preliminary secret experiments, Stalin made the momentous decision which was to change the lives of millions of people, both in the countryside and the cities, within and outside of the Soviet Union, for generations to come. He gave orders for accelerated, forced, total (*splosh-naya*) collectivization of the peasants. The immediate consequences of the collectivization drives, which caught the Russian countryside in several devastating whirlwinds during the early 1930's, have never been precisely calculated. Ten million people dispossessed and deported is one of the most recent scholarly estimates, which has the added authority of being Stalin's own figure, frankly admitted to Winston Churchill on the fingers of his hands. Many, perhaps most, of these millions were not killed, imprisoned, or exiled; outcasts on the land, they migrated to the cities and the new factories. It was Soviet Russia's grim recapitulation of the enclosure movement in England and the transatlantic migration to America's industrial cities. How many hundreds of thousands—or millions—starved to death on the road to exile, froze to death stuffed into wintry freight cars, were shot by the OGPU, or died in labor camps, may never be known. Nor would it be easy to count the thousands of orphaned small children, offspring of peasants, who became emaciated vagabonds on the roads and in the towns of Russia, or to calculate the vast economic and spiritual waste therein involved. Other figures are more precise; for example, half of Russia's livestock were slaugtered by hostile peasants. Agricultural and dairy production declined by a fifth. The government's power to obtain its procurement requirements meant starvation for many, and in 1933, helped to bring about one of the most devastating famines in all human history, in which millions more lost their lives. The pyramid of corpses was piled higher once again in the latter part of the decade, when millions more died in the Great Purges, for which the collectivization must be considered a primary cause.

The motives which prompted Stalin's decision to collectivize are very complex, and to this day have not been fully weighed and assessed, although a vigorous debate still pursues this historic and terrible act. How great a determinant was ideology—the soviet Marxist goal (already delayed for over a decade) of the building of socialism and the destruction of capitalism in agriculture? Was the economic problem of more importance to a pragmatist like Stalin? Did he contemplate the need for more agricultural production and higher procurements, which, in his view, could only be achieved on large, mechanized plantations —the replacements for Russia's twenty-four million small, primitive, subsistence-level farms? The political problems emphasized by official sources and by Stalin himself at the time were the growing power of the kulaks, the "treason" of the party's right wing and its supporters, and the threat of foreign, capitalist intervention, bent on destroying the economically and militarily weak first fortress of communist power. How serious were these threats? Was Stalin acting primarily as an oriental despot, in the old Muscovite and Petrine tradition of forced modernization for war through regimentation of the peasant masses? Or was he simply carried along by events from which he believed he could not retreat and which he was obsessively impelled to push to a total resolution?

Stalin himself gave no answers to these questions, only contradictory hints. He told his people that he was constructing a "socialist society." He warned the party that he was fighting a gigantic, interwoven plot in the villages, factories, laboratories, and government echelons, which was bent on blocking the development of this society. He explained to Winston Churchill that it was economically necessary to uproot the stubborn backwardness of the Russian peasant. He made no secret of his admiration for Ivan the Terrible, who did not hesitate to use violence to break the resistance of "unprogressive" groups who stood in his way, or his respect for Peter the Great, the cruel despot who first worked to modernize Russia.

The answers which historians and economists have provided to explain the decision to collectivize have not been much clearer than Stalin's hints. Scholars have both asserted and questioned whether collectivization was the correct socialist solution, or good economics, or politically urgent. Some see it as a logical response, called for by the conditions of the time; others condemn it as a desperate gamble, an obsessive, ignorant, and cruel act. For some observers, Stalin was leaping into the communist future; for others, he was returning to the feudal-military past.

This controversial subject will be debated for generations.[1] Some aspects relative to Russia's economic growth seem clear. From the vantage point of industrialization policy, it was not the collective farm in itself, efficient or inefficient, socialistic or un-socialistic, necessary or unnecessary, that was crucial to Stalin's plans, but the system of money and labor tribute to the state that was developed simultaneously and based upon the collective organization. This insured the government the desired supply of food, raw materials, and saleable crops, independent of peasant savings, consumption, or reluctance to grow, independent of technical and organizational efficiency, and, indeed, independent of the weather itself. It was the peasants, now, and not the com-missars, who would have to tremble when the crops failed. Such a system of tribute was hardly based on socialist tenets, nor was it dependent on raising the level of production. It was essentially a system of taxation combined with one of forced labor. In the NEP period, the peasants produced first for their own consump-tion and then sold the surplus on the free market to the state. Now they would produce primarily for the state; what was left after the state took its share was their own. However, they were now obliged both to work and to pay; they could no longer resist government taxation by refusing to pay, to market, to work, or to grow. If there were any precedents for Stalin's system of tribute, they were not to be found in the history of socialist ideas, but rather in old Russian serf obligations of *obrok* and *barshchina*, or, more recently, the grain export policies of the tsarist Ministers of Finance.

Like the "system" of Vyshnegradsky and Witte in the 1890's, the Stalinist tribute was a way of industrializing Russia at the expense of the peasantry. How specifically was a large segment of the income of the Russian peasant transformed into capital investment? The process began with the obligatory delivery of grain and other produce, required after 1932 from every collec-tive farm. Prior to this, the entire crop had been purchased at prefixed low prices through a system of "contracts." This method

[1] See Bibliography for Chapter 4 for a listing of this literature.

of payment was found unreliable, and was replaced by a more direct levy. A nominal price was paid for produce requisitioned, but this was so far below the cost of production, that obligatory deliveries were in effect a tax in kind, or, more precisely (as was argued by some soviet theorists at the time), a form of rent. In the late 1930's, obligatory deliveries amounted to about 15 percent of the grain harvest, the most important of Russia's crops. This quota, adjusted by the state, had to be met before all other distributions of the crop. In the early days of the new system, armed force was sometimes used to insure delivery of the agricultural tribute. The next slice—from 15 to 20 percent—was taken by the government as payment for the use of state machinery. That this rental far exceeded the costs of the Machine Tractor Stations that Stalin set up to service groups of collective farms can be seen in the extra charge of 15 percent of the crop that was levied on those *kolkhozy* that did not use machinery. Then came smaller assessments from each collective's barns for milling, the rates of which were much higher than those of private millers of tsarist days, and which brought to the government more than a million tons of grain in extra revenue during the late 1930's. *Kolkhozy* indebted to the government made additional small payments from the yearly crop. The government, thus, carried off about a third of the harvest before the peasants in the collective farm saw anything. When we add to this the small percentages of grain withheld by the *kolkhoz* and the state for various services, and high retail prices established for industrial goods sold in the countryside, it appears that the peasant worked full time for the collective farm for about 60 percent pay; i.e., when all the government requisitioning was completed, about three fifths of the crop was left for the people who grew it.

Actually, the peasant did not spend all of his time working for the collective. If he had been obliged to do this, very probably he and many urban dwellers would have starved. Peasant evasion of work on the collective brought two responses from the government during the 1930's—one coercive, the other conciliatory. To force him to work the minimum amount of time deemed necessary to make the *kolkhoz* productive, a fixed number of work days out of each year was established. In theory under this system, the peasant was obliged to work for the collective from dawn to dusk for about nine months annually. In practice, he worked less. However, he could not evade fixed norms of labor under strict penalty. As in the days of the tough old Russian capitalist, Timofei Morozov, absenteeism and inefficiency were punished with fines. The wages of the collective farmers were calculated on the basis of the "workday" (*trudoden*). The *trudoden* was not compensation for a day's labor, but rather a rate of pay for piece work which varied greatly according to skill. It also constituted a dividend from the crop that remained to *kolkhoz* members each year after seed reserves were taken, and was thus determined by the size of the crop.

In addition to sharing the group return, the *kolkhoz* could sell about 5 percent of the crop at higher prices, a fund which was then turned over to the members, although not before an income tax was paid. For about one hundred days a year, the peasant was permitted cultivation of his own plot of land, the produce of which he could consume or sell in free markets for competitive prices. Although the government closely regulated the sizes of these farms, they brought in over half the income of the average peasant in the late 1930's. However, a relatively high income tax was levied on such gains, an imposition designed to discourage the growth of peasant enterprises. In the final analysis, through a system of direct taxes and outright requisitions, high prices for goods and services and exceedingly low or even nominal prices for agricultural produce, the government was able to extract about a quarter of the wealth of the Russian peasantry.

The agricultural produce levy, together with the other taxes extracted from the peasant and the higher prices tagged on the manufactured goods he was permitted to buy, was a way of drastically curtailing his purchases of consumer goods. This system was instituted to insure not only that peasant income would be diverted into industrialization, but also that most of the very limited supply of consumer goods would be reserved for the cities. In the early five year plans, when rationing was in effect, this discrimination was more direct: such goods were simply not made available to the peasants.

The produce tax was levied in the second instance on state crop-requisitioning agencies, and ultimately on the consumer. The funds so derived, over and above agricultural products used to feed the army, passed into the state budget. Well over a fifth of the yearly revenue (in 1938), or about twenty-seven billion rubles, came from the turnover tax on socialized agriculture, the incidence of which fell largely on the peasants. During the same year, twenty-three billion was invested in industry, mostly in the form of grants to new and expanding enterprises. In effect, the peasant footed most of the bill for the industrialization of Russia under Stalin, although he was not the only one to make sacrifices.

The consumer was the next link in the Stalinist system of capital formation. In addition to appropriating a lion's share of the annual crop, the state transformed the largest part of consumer purchases by means of the "turnover tax" (*sbor s oborota*) into a fund of billions of rubles for industrial investment. The turnover tax was the most important feature of a radical fiscal reform introduced several months after the first collectivization drive. These new regulations of 1930 swept away the cumbersome existing tax structure. The turnover tax was as important a mechanism of the Stalinist system of industrialization as the collectivization, and, in a sense, was its fiscal counterpart. However, this "tax" was more than just a very complex device for obtaining revenue. It was a system of price control or, more generally, a reflection in the price structure of an economy absolutely controlled by a state pursuing a policy of diversion of a major portion of national resources into the construction of heavy industry. In a country still primarily agricultural, although possessing a relatively substantial consumer industry, this meant a transferral of wealth from the agricultural to the industrial sector of the economy and the restriction of consumption. As the Soviet economy during the First Five Year Plan was shifted massively in the direction of heavy industrialization, the number of wage earners engaged in the new industrial effort, from steel workers to professors of technology, rapidly increased, while at the same time

and with equal haste, production in consumer industries was curtailed. A depression of wages and rationing—both policies being
implemented during the early years of the Stalinist industrialization—could not prevent a high rise in prices of consumer goods
together with a growing demand for these goods on the part of
people who were able to pay. The difference between the cost of
production, transport, and marketing of consumer goods and the
retail price soon became very great. This difference, calculated in
a number of ways, was collected at frequent intervals from the
various state requisitioning, wholesaling, and retailing agencies
as the turnover tax. Until the 1950's (except for the period of the
Second World War), the turnover tax was the largest source of
state revenue, usually bringing in from over half to two thirds of
total budgetary receipts.

Not only a reflection in the price system of a planned economy diverting most of its resources into heavy industry and restricting consumption, the turnover tax had many other functions.
It could be used as a system of controls to stimulate areas of
industry or agriculture through manipulation of the price system.
It could operate to restrict consumption of a particular product.
Thus, state farms could be favored by measures which enabled
them to buy manufactured goods at lower prices than the *kolkhozy;* the turnover tax on vodka was used, similar to the policies
of other countries, for purposes of both temperance and revenue,
and was usually very high—84 percent of the final sale price at
the beginning of the Second World War.

The urban consumer's contribution to the industrialization
drive did not end with the turnover tax, exorbitant as it was.
Like the peasant, he paid other taxes, some of which were hidden.
Income taxes, retained from the NEP, were emphasized and increased in the last decade of Stalin's rule. This type of tax, at its
peak, brought in a very small portion of total revenue compared
to the turnover tax (less than 10 percent).[2] Nevertheless, income taxes came to constitute an additional burden for the
majority of the urban population, apart from the utterly indigent,

[2] Other minor sources of revenue and investment funds were the profits
tax levied on state enterprises and a tax on savings bank deposits.

who were not taxed (or soldiers and students, largely exempted from income tax). The tax rate changed from group to group. Although progressively scaled for some categories, income taxes were not in their overall incidence really progressive. The "rich" in certain groups paid very high taxes, but others who earned high incomes were taxed at almost the same rate as ordinary industrial laborers. The middle-income group—owners of small shops, artists, and professional people charging fees—were relatively heavily taxed. The average factory worker in 1954 paid an income tax of 938 rubles, or 12 percent of his wages—a big bite, but one which represented a rate only 1 percent lower than, say, the director of the entire textile industry, even if the latter earned, as was possible, thirty times as much.

Industrial workers paid a much smaller income tax during the early years of the Stalin industrialization drive (about 2.6 percent for the average household in 1937). Income taxes in the early 1930's were not designed to obtain revenue or curtail consumption so much as to discriminate against groups who were symbols of the old order and individuals receiving income from private activities, such as the clergy and shopkeepers. The real wages of industrial workers were so low during the first and second five year plans—at a time when even money wages were being depressed—that extensive direct taxation was not feasible. The government, to compel further savings, had to resort to another form of covert taxation above and beyond the turnover tax. This was done primarily through floating—or rather, levying—domestic loans. Heavy pressure (including a drastic currency devaluation of 90 percent in 1947 to liquidate a repressed inflation and to discipline wartime cash hoarders) was applied to wage earners to goad them into investment of any savings and surpluses. Most often, however, this came in the form of compulsory purchase of government bonds, which were paid for by regular salary deductions. This pressure proved to be so effective that all of the fifteen issues from 1928 to 1941, except two, were oversubscribed. Bonds were not redeemable until maturity, a date which was moved ahead several times by government decree, until it stretched over two decades. As the years moved on, the bonds depreciated. Their value was further reduced by a number of conversions, in which the interest was cut from 10 to 2 percent. These manipulations, together with the coercive conditions surrounding the sale of the bonds, have led some economists to consider soviet domestic loans of the Stalin era a form of taxation. This covert tax absorbed between 1.4 and 5.4 percent of the annual money income of a soviet household in peacetime years.

The total burden of the various levies imposed upon the Russian urban consumer during the period of Stalinist industrialization has been estimated at between half and two thirds of personal money income.[3] This was an even higher proportion than what was taken from the peasants, although it did not represent a greater imposition, since the level of the peasants' income was much lower. However, money taxation has to be weighed with the less tangible and measurable rewards and sacrifices that became the boon and the lot of the soviet worker, that is, social services and benefits, changes in the standard of living, and fluctuations of real wages.

The income which he lost through direct taxes and bond purchases was regained to some extent through free social benefits. The most important of such benefits were old-age and survivors pensions, sickness and maternity allowances, as well as those educational and medical services for which no fees were charged. Excluding the war years (when the reverse was true), such benefits exceeded tax and bond payments. According to a recent computation,[4] this social wage in 1937 and 1940 exceeded direct taxes by approximately 550 to 250 percent. The imbalance diminished as taxes rose after the war. Deducting for the social insurance mark-up (a payroll tax on enterprises which was added to the price of their products), we still obtain a balance of social wages over income taxes and bond purchases of well above 200 percent in the 1930's. However, this figure must be modified by allowance for restrictions which were placed on benefit payments, and whatever approximate measurement can be made of

[3] Holzman's estimate. See Bibliography.
[4] Chapman. See Bibliography.

such intangibles as the extent and quality of medical and educational services.

Similarly, the deterioration of the standard of living, resulting from the restriction of consumption upon which the industrialization drive was predicated, must also be estimated. This can be done most concretely for the housing crisis. During the first decade of the plan era over twenty-five million people moved into Russia's cities. Most of this vast and sudden migration was to industrial centers. The new urban dwellers did not substantially sacrifice income by the payment of rent, as in Western countries. Soviet rents and utilities costs remained low compared to many European countries, and were well below half of such costs in the United States. In the mid-1930's these costs were about 10 percent of the average working family's income. However, adequate housing simply was not provided. Construction of private housing (except for hand-made shanty towns) practically ceased after 1929. Investment in public housing was cut to the bone; what was put up did not even begin to meet the needs of the mushrooming urban mass. Similar to the policies of many countries in modern times, adequate housing for the poor was given a very low priority in the scale of economic needs. In Stalinist Russia, heavy industry came first, although provision was made for more than substantial housing of the more privileged members of the new elite. The result was the very rapid development of slum conditions.

For the least fortunate, such as peasants newly arrived from the countryside, vagrants from semiprimitive minority groups, and other unskilled workers, this meant living in tents, underground dugouts (*zemlyanki*) or hovels on the outskirts of cities, built of industrial scrap and mud. As late as 1938, according to one observer, over 50,000 persons, or one fourth of the population of Magnitogorsk (the new Urals steel center) were living in such squalid conditions. Another 110,000 lived in barracks, each of which might house hundreds of individuals and families in extremely crowded conditions. A fortunate minority had access to apartments of prerevolutionary or socialist vintage. Here overcrowding was also the rule, as everywhere in Russia. By 1950, the average habitation density was four individuals to a room. This was far less than the crisis situation of the 1930's, which was intensified by wartime destruction and migration, but constituted about half the living space available in 1913. Prior to the end of the Second World War, there was little central heating, plumbing, or electricity to be found in these socialist slums, and no privacy. Public housing construction that did take place during the Stalin era was mostly of the communal type of apartment house, with kitchens and baths shared by several families. The design was dictated not by social ideals, but by economic considerations.

The sacrifices imposed on the soviet worker in the industrialization drive and again in the war can be seen most clearly, from an economic point of view, in the sharp decline of real wages. The fluctuations of real wages during the Stalin era are not easy to determine or verify, and few of the figures that have been advanced are accepted without dispute. This confusion has been occasioned, not only because the soviet government exaggerated its claims and made some essential statistics secret after 1930, but also because of several intangibles, none of them measurable without difficulty, that must be taken into account to arrive at sound and fully qualified approximations. Thus, the components of a true soviet real wage for Stalin's time consist not only of the relationship of wages to prices, but equally of such divergent factors as the proper value of the soviet welfare system, the extent of private income derived from vegetable gardens and farm animals owned by peasants and urban dwellers as well, the savings provided by government nurseries for the small children of workers, the increase in the number of wage earners in the family unit, and the dislocations of war.

A valid geographical and historical context for comparative statistics is also required. Although soviet real wages in the mid-1930's dropped to the incredible depth of about 24 percent of real wages in the United States, they were only a small fraction lower than those in less industrialized countries, like Chile or Italy, and above those of the fellaheen and coolies of the underdeveloped Orient. On the other hand, many of the social services, which Soviet economists with much exaggeration claimed to be equivalent to a third of the total money wages (in the 1950's) were also functioning, and in some cases providing superior benefits, in other countries. Within the Russian context alone, real wages had a catastrophic decline after 1928. At the ebb points during the First Five Year Plan and the war, they were half the 1928 level, which was not regained until the early 1950's.

The main causes for the drop between 1928 and 1931 were the rapid rise of consumer prices and the cost of living created by the industrialization effort. The disappearance of most consumer goods was met initially by five years of rationing. Once again, as on the eve of the February Revolution, Russia became the land of endless bread lines. The recovery of real wages was painfully slow in the 1930's. By 1938, they did not yet exceed 50 percent of the level of a decade before. One reason for this was the policy, rigorously pursued during the industrialization drive, of depressing money wages. These wages lagged far behind prices, and pay raises were kept lower than increases in productivity. The exception to this rule, as in the case of housing, were skilled workers and members of the new intelligentsia and officialdom, who were rewarded with substantially higher wages. During the war, vacations were cancelled, the work day was extended in practice from seven and eight to ten and eleven hours, and the work week grew from five to six days. Inflation consumed much of the extra income accrued by this punishing work schedule. Real wages dropped again. Pressures were exerted on workers through the various command levers established over them. Factory managers bullied their employees into working long hours. The trade unions, whose primary function in the industrialization drive was to discipline and train the new labor force, launched attacks on any agitation for higher wages among their members, and were opposed to both striking and quitting.

These pressures were the milder manifestations of a general tendency in Soviet labor policy toward stricter regulation and the intensified use of force. The immediate and urgent economic cause for tightening-up was the appearance of acute labor shortages in the factories. This phenomenon both accompanied and directly resulted from the collectivization and industrialization drives. Cancelling out the vast migration to the cities of dispossessed peasants was another massive exodus to the villages of those hoping not to be dispossessed. The shrinkage of the industrial work force was worsened by an abnormal labor turnover characteristic of the early plan era. Low wages and poor housing conditions had reduced the average term of employment in some industries to a few months, as workers wandered from factory to factory in search of a better living. In scenes reminiscent of the formative period of Muscovite serfdom, some workers were enticed away from jobs by ambitious plant managers.

The government met this labor crisis with a mobilization of the Russian working force that resembled and in some ways surpassed the enserfment of the peasantry in tsarist times. As in the sixteenth and seventeenth centuries, voluntary indentures gave way to mandatory ones; and in 1940, term contracts (for skilled workers) were replaced by compulsory indeterminate tenure. Internal passports and harsh penalties for fugitives prevented Stalin's workers from moving, as they had done for the serfs of Peter the Great; and the soviet government, like its predecessor, could transfer workers at will and conscript others for essential tasks. During the Second World War, labor corvées for local construction work and harvesting were imposed. Although not as heavy as the labor obligations on tsarist estates, or on the collective farms, a *barshchina* of approximately three to ten weeks per annum had to be met. Labor mobilization, however, was far more total than any the Russian people had hitherto experienced. Juvenile labor was utilized extensively for harvest levies, while young boys, barely in their teens, were trained and placed in factory work. An entire new female proletariat was created: by the end of the First Five Year Plan, women had come to make up a fifth of the industrial labor force.

Discipline in the Stalinist industrial system was far less barbaric and more democratic than the punishments meted out under serfdom. Unlike the privileged elite of bygone times, the managers of soviet factories suffered the same stern military regimen as was imposed on the workers. It was they who enforced the rules, under draconic penalty for lack of vigilance and rigorousness. Absenteeism and even lateness of the employees were subject to criminal prosecution and heavy fines.

The development of forced labor on a vast scale was not so much a carry-over of tsarist traditions as it was both cause and effect of the industrialization drive. The tsars had used convict labor for construction work; but prior to 1917—as well as in the NEP period—the number of convicts constituted only a small fraction of the manpower put in chains under Stalin. The liquidation of the kulaks and the great purges—the two holocausts from which most of the slave labor was derived in the 1930's—had many complex causes, which (like those of the collectivization) have long been debated. Although the industrialization drive and the disruptions and sacrifices which it entailed were undoubtedly a primary cause of the various purges, it is not easy to isolate the economic foundations of the forced labor system. Millions of people were not arrested out of purely economic calculations to provide slaves for work projects. Nor could a system of such magnitude, cost, and economic significance have been maintained for a generation purely as a matter of political caprice or despotic obsession on the parts of Stalin and the NKVD. Very great numbers of people became slave laborers in camps and settlements all over the Soviet Union for largely political reasons. The real or pretended threat of opposition to government policy and to the police was the cause for most arrests; and in the final manhunt of the *Yezhovshchina,* the fears and fanaticism of the policemen themselves became a factor.

The same official indifference to human life and suffering that had led to the deprivation of freedom for millions of convicts also led to indifference in economic considerations for the disposition of this huge pool of labor. There were few instances where slave labor was crucial to the industrialization drive, and it was frequently squandered. The profitability of this primitive system, in the final balance of liabilities and profits, is seen by most scholars to have been negligible—about 4 percent of the total annual capital investment, according to one estimate. Nevertheless, it performed a number of important economic functions in the industrialization program. It became a powerful vested interest, and, increasingly, an essential part of the soviet economic and social system. Whatever motives were involved in expanding Russia's convict force from a few hundred thousand in 1928 to a peak of several million a decade later, it must have become apparent very quickly that the cost of maintaining, transporting, and securing such large numbers in unproductive or only partially productive incarceration would have been astronomical, and would have seriously distracted from the industrialization effort. According to calculations based on the testimony of former high ranking officers of the NKVD, the total costs for some seven million soviet slaves in 1941, if they had not paid their own way, would have ranged from about twenty-five to thirty-six billion rubles, or from 50 to 72 percent of the total capital investment of that year. These people, unlike the army of guards, were living on the very margin of human subsistence. As the number of arrests climbed into the millions, Stalin and his police chieftains, in effect, had to choose among the alternatives of liberation, massacre, or exploitation of their prisoners, whichever means best sufficed to drastically minimize their cost. Stalin was fully capable of mass clemency or mass murder (both of which he demonstrated to his Polish prisoners, to give the most striking example). For most of the inhabitants of his concentration camps, however, he chose the alternative of slave labor—a fate involving hideous suffering and privation, a path across Russia's northern and eastern wastes littered with millions of graves, the destruction of some of the most productive, educated, and liberal elements of the soviet people, and the creation of a social system which, like those of most slave societies, resulted in the brutalization of the ruling class and the emergence at the bottom of the social scale of a large caste of ostracized, degraded, and servile humanity.

The idea of exploiting convict labor for the industrialization drive developed at the beginning of the First Five Year Plan. The central administration of the prison camps (GULAG), an agency of the NKVD, was assigned special tasks, while quotas were set for its contributions to the Plan. It was also obliged to supply labor for factories and other state undertakings. Most prisoners were used in mining, logging, or construction work—heavy, unskilled labor from which the maximum of profit could be derived from the exploitation of large masses of human hands and backs, virtually unaided by machinery of any kind. Thus, hundreds of thousands of diggers were put to work excavating canals and building railroads, creating scenes reminiscent of the public works projects of Peter the Great or the railroad poems of Nekrasov. However, a large number of slaves, perhaps as high as a million, were assigned to factories operated directly by state agencies or by the police. This type of employment ranged widely —from experimental atomic plants to handicraft workshops where female prisoners made ornamental wooden boxes. Large numbers of prisoners were moved long distances at frequent intervals, as the slave camp literature abundantly testifies. Slave labor could more easily and profitably be utilized in the development of the barren and frozen Siberian extremities of the Soviet Union, although transport costs were high, and life, labor, and funds were sometimes squandered on useless, wasteful, and grandiose economic monuments in the northern darkness and snow.

The size of the camp population at its peak in the late 1930's testifies to its economic significance. Guesses lacking any real substantiation range from two to forty million. The figure of eight to nine million in 1938 and 1939 seems to attract the widest agreement of experts. Although the profitability of this form of slavery was small, this was because of the high costs of transport and security, not those of food, care, and shelter. In terms of diet, disease, and exposure, prisoners were kept at the borderline of life and death, and minimal food rations were based on productivity. If the prisoner-sustenance expenses alone had been deducted from the receipts of the forced labor system, the profit balance would have been enormous.

Nevertheless, its importance to the Stalinist industrial system was undeniable. As the scope of GULAG enterprises and projects widened, while the number of deaths rapidly multiplied, labor replacement, as elsewhere in the soviet economy, became more and more essential, if quotas were to be met and projects completed. Manpower considerations, although the evidence is fragmentary, must have come to exert a growing influence on police arrests and convictions. It is clear that few pardons were granted in this period; and the idea of expiration of sentence became a fiction.

Slave labor served other very important functions in the industrialization drive. The government had greater control over its mobility than with the chronically migratory free labor force, despite the increasing restrictions placed on the ordinary worker. Slaves were practically self-sufficient and could be kept, or sent, where needed with dispatch. Mass arrests over short periods of time—two or more million a year after 1932—not only ended the underemployment of labor resources in Russia's villages, but also operated to curb inflation. Curtailment of the income of consumers, the traditional remedy for rising prices and which was already being rigorously applied, was supplemented by the forcible removal of large numbers of consumers from the market. The labor camp system was thus another means, and the most drastic of all, of curtailing consumption for the purpose of diverting resources into the development of heavy industry. The removal of such pressures on the consumer market played a role in facilitating wage improvements and the end of rationing for industrial workers in the mid-1930's. Thus, the harsh exploitation of 130 million peasants and several million slaves lightened the burden for the more privileged minority of fifty-odd million urban workers, and the far smaller number that formed the technical and bureaucratic elite.

Force was the primary instrument of soviet labor policy during the Stalin era. However, as in tsarist days and the period of the Civil War, the impressment of manpower into factory employment and government construction projects, and even the exploitation of convict labor, competed at times with patriotic enthusiasm and wage inducements as goads to the work force. The stick of coercion alternated with the carrot of material incentives, but the abundant wells of Russian idealism could also be tapped. Massive doses of propaganda could be used to stimulate this idealism, or to counterfeit it. People could be inspired to greater efforts, but failing that, could be forced to "emulate" contrived achievements.

All the resources of the communications media in soviet Russia were enrolled in the task of propagandizing the industrialization drive. After 1928, poets and novelists, like peasants and shock workers in the factories, were mobilized into brigades. Their collective task was to extol the five year plans, revile their enemies, and do this simply and quickly. Similar subject matter was introduced into the theatre: directors and actors were called upon to portray dramatically the struggle between communists and "wreckers" in the industrialization program, and also to show the conversion of the intelligentsia to the camp of the industrializers. Musical composers were ordered to write "mass songs" for wide circulation on the radio. Military tempos and simple soothing melodies were designed to promote government campaigns, while lyrics extolled industrial and agricultural achievements. The great soviet film directors of the 1920's era retained more freedom than many of their contemporaries in the other arts, but were obliged to turn out their share of industrialization melodramas and patriotic historical epics. A complete and mobile motion picture studio, consisting of three railroad cars, went around the Soviet Union in the early 1930's making educational films and documentaries on location. However, most of the creations of the soviet cinematographers in the early plan era, like those of the painters and novelists, were insipid propaganda, although a few works of distinction appeared. A spirit of excitement and optimism was created by writers like Katayev, but how much this reflected, affected, or disguised economic reality is difficult to determine.

Nowhere was the Stalinist blending of propaganda, industriousness, sacrifice, and compulsion better displayed than in the Stakhanovite movement, launched in 1935. Stakhanovism had its precursor in the "Communist Saturdays" of the Civil War period (see Chapter 3), which had never been of great economic significance, but had left a favorable impression. At the commencement of the Stalinist industrialization drive, it was decided to revive this patriotic idealism in the form of "Socialist Emulation." Socialist Emulation was designed as a form of competition for factory labor, in which highly motivated "shock workers" (*udar-*

niki) would expend extra efforts and, conversely, restrain themselves from loafing on the job. Such exhortations did not work, and the encouragement of outstanding workers was soon reversed to a system of vigilance and denunciation against shirkers. Material enticements were quickly introduced, although these tended to come in the form of special privileges and rewards for groups, rather than pay increases for individuals.

In August, 1935, a miner in the Don Basin by the name of Aleksei Stakhanov set a fantastic work record for the cutting of coal. In one shift, he was able to drill away almost fifteen times the amount of coal previously averaged by individual workers. Stakhanov did not accomplish this seemingly prodigious feat through superhuman physical efforts, but by organizing an efficient division of labor among his teammates. Stakhanov did all the cutting; the others performed all the auxiliary tasks. Thus, the average increased productivity of the group was far less than the phenomenal figures advertised in the soviet press, about 70, not 1500 percent—still a remarkable improvement.

Stakhanov's feat was given immediate, nationwide publicity. Stakhanovites soon appeared in other industries and in agriculture, following similar methods of efficient reorganization of work. They too achieved overnight fame. Whether the movement was spontaneous, as the government asserted, or a promotional stunt, cynically manipulated and received, is an open question. Stakhanov's original performance, staged in the presence of the local mine superintendent, party boss, and newspaper editor, was probably arranged by higher authorities. But it was clearly an exciting idea, and the prospect of substantial rewards on the basis of efficient innovation, rather than sweating, soon attracted a large following. This naturally led to abuses, but such instances of fraudulent competitions which slowed down production, were overbalanced by general increases in efficiency.

The government's initial purpose in promoting the Stakhanovite movement was revealed in the order of December, 1935, which upgraded all work norms. Quotas were raised again, two years later. Stakhanovism was, thus, in the first instance, a promotional campaign to prepare the ground for the extension of work quotas. Those workers who would not or could not become more efficient would simply have to work harder, or earn less. In this sense, it is correct to characterize Stakhanovism as a "mixture of progressive rationalization and old time sweated labour." (Deutscher). A number of soviet workers must have believed this, when they reacted to the movement by beating up and even murdering Stakhanovites. But Stakhanovism was also designed to provide generous rewards in the form of substantial pay increases and other benefits for those workers who possessed the intelligence and initiative to effectively utilize their time and equipment. Soon there were not just the heroic Stakhanovs, Vinogradovas, and others, but over a million Stakhanovites, whose standard of living was considerably higher than that of Russian labor's rank and file. Stakhanov himself eventually became an official in the Coal Ministry. This elite developed a stake in the Stalinist industrial system, as the mass of less enterprising workers became poorer and resentful. Thus, in its social aspect, the Stakhanov movement might best be characterized as a form of industrial Stolypinism (see Chapter 2).

It may be concluded that it was through historically conventional means of reward and exploitation that Stalin accumulated capital and mobilized labor for the industrialization drive of the 1930's. The creation of economic elites, a heavy tribute taken from the peasantry, forced savings imposed on the consumer through high prices and taxes, the depression of industrial wages, the imposition of longer working hours and a severe discipline of the working force, the enslavement of large numbers of people for use in heavy construction projects, the convict colonization of backward, colonial fringe lands—all this was similar to what the tsars and the capitalists of Western Europe had done. What was unique in Stalin's method was the unparalleled application of force which resulted from the rapid pace of development demanded and maintained by the Soviet leadership.

Stalin's economic policies toward the non-Russian nationalities and the Eastern European countries which came under Russian influence at the end of the Second World War also represent a continuity with tsarist and European imperialist traditions, as well as another harsh and exploitative means for the accumulation of industrial capital. "Colonial plundering," condemned by socialist economists from Marx to Preobrazhensky, was never as important for soviet economic development as it was for the industrialization of some European countries. The acquisition of reparation funds, slave labor, industrial equipment, and the confiscation of assets from Germany, Austria, and the Eastern European satellites, not to exclude the highly discriminatory trade system imposed on that area in the decade after the war, come closest to approximating old-style colonialism. Estimates on the tremendous profits thereby accrued by Russia (through the same system we have seen operative in the collective farm system—of buying at low prices) are as high as twenty-two billion rubles a year. One educated guess (Jasny) is that 10 percent of soviet post-war investment in reconstruction and development, and an equal proportion of the labor force engaged in the production of material goods, came from Eastern European sources.

Russia's economic relations with the non-Russian nationalities of the Soviet Union during the Stalin era is more difficult to measure, because it was not so much one of trade and tribute as of a more generally inequitable relationship between metropolis and colony, favoring the former. The most striking example of this variant of modern imperialism was Uzbekistan, possessing the fourth largest national group in the Soviet Union. The relationship of Uzbekistan to Russia under Stalin bears valid analogies to that of Egypt with England in the heyday of imperialism. The main contribution of this backward Moslem nation to the soviet industrialization drive consisted of the vastly increased production of cotton fibre for the Russian textile industry, to the detriment of the economic development of the colonial area. Some modernization was fostered in Uzbek cities, which became the industrial hub of Russian Central Asia. But the urban industrial elite came to consist of Russian immigrants, while unskilled labor and agricultural work was reserved for Uzbek natives. Some of these migrated to factory work elsewhere in the Soviet Union. During the same period, Russian colonization and disruption of primitive native economies occurred in the development of the

far eastern regions. The extent to which Russian industry bene-
fited from these colonial relationships must be balanced, as in the
case of European imperialism, against the substantial industrial
and cultural development that occurred under soviet auspices.
Similarly, it would be difficult to calculate the extent to which
the economic interests of such large and more developed nations
as the Ukraine were sacrificed to the industrialization of the Urals
and Siberia, and the role of strategic over imperialist considerations in the reapportionment of investment.

The most original aspect of the Stalinist method of industrialization was the planning system, and it is under its popular
name—*pyatilyetka,* the five year plan—that his industrialization
program has gone down in history. Large-scale planning did
not in fact function as a magical panacea which enabled Russia to
avoid the gluts, crises, unemployment, and other irregularities
observed in market economies, as Stalin nevertheless advertised
and many people believed at the time. Nor did planning prevent
serious slumps and other irrationalities of a different order in the
soviet economy during the plan era. The soviet "plan," as it
actually functioned, may be described as a statistical expression
and projection of the almost total bureaucratization of the nation's
economic life for the purpose of forced economic development; a
guidebook, as it were, for the huge apparatus which administered
Stalinist industrialization. As such, it was not so much "the little
child of socialism," as a magnification of institutions and practices
deeply rooted in the Russian tradition. The idea of a planned
economy, however, had also become part of soviet socialist thinking, originating with Lenin's admiration of German wartime planning, and carrying through plan GOELRO and other largely paper projections of the 1920's (see Chapter 3). The social and
economic cataclysm of the collectivization transformed soviet
planning from "flights of thought" (as one of the earlier plans had
been described) to a workable system of industrial administration. Collectivization obliterated most of the vast private sector
of the NEP structure. This destruction of a market economy
necessitated the building of a new system which could substitute
for the workings of the "invisible hand" of prices and profits as a

way of allocating national resources. The decision to collectivize once again activated forces far beyond the sphere of agriculture —in this instance, the growth of a huge administrative apparatus capable of estimating and coordinating funds, manpower, and natural resources on a scale unparalleled in human history. The plan must also be considered—like the other major aspects of the soviet industrialization drive—a reflection of Stalin: of his intelligence, his ideals, his character, his obsessions, and his miscalculations. For Stalin was the ultimate planner. It was Stalin in the end who gave the directives to the planners.

There were, of course, many kinds of plans and many functions of these plans. The larger plans at certain times were synchronized with practical industrial administration, but usually served essentially propaganda purposes—to extol in exaggerated figures the economic potential and achievements of soviet Russia, or, for internal consumption, to goad industrial management into greater productive efforts. The long-range plan has been most aptly described as a "hypothèse de croissance" (Zaleski). The most famous of these, the six *pyatilyetki,* were largely desiderata of this kind, as were the even longer plans projected after Stalin's death. This "perspective planning," as the Russians called it, is no longer recognized by many economists to have functioned in any real administrative or economic sense. Although Stalin described his plans as the law of the land, their figures were not in fact used as a basis for orders or contracts, although some attempt at adjustment to solid statistical reality has been observed after 1956. Realistic and functional planning did take place from the very beginning, as it does today, on a year-to-year basis or for even shorter periods of time. Perhaps it would be most accurate to view this short-range, operational plan, not as a scientific forecast, but rather, as a kind of statistical index, under continuing revision, of an immensely complex and constantly changing administration, embracing practically the entire economic life of the nation.

This bureaucratic system of economic growth came to involve not only the vast network of economic agencies that mushroomed in Russia during the early stages of the industrialization drive, but ultimately, the entire apparatus of soviet political life. Planning at various levels could become the concern of the secret police (who had their own economic departments), state controllers, and public prosecutors, as well as plant management and statistical agencies—and, of course, the Communist Party. It will suffice here to summarize the main features of the system as these influenced the industrialization process.[5]

Operational or "administrative" planning, usually done on an annual basis, began with general directives. These came, not from statisticians or economists, but from the Politbureau, and ultimately from Stalin. Stalin sought the advice of Russia's leading economists, but apparently did not follow their views on crucial issues, when they disagreed with his, and at the beginning of the industrialization drive, repudiated them in characteristic fashion. The most important economist in Gosplan, who opposed the early industrialization plans for having unrealistically high goals and being dangerously disproportionate in the allocation of investment, were purged in a series of trials in 1930.

Stalin's concept of planning was not that of an economist—a science in which it is generally recognized, he had little training or interest—but rather, the approach of a revolutionary and a bureaucrat. His experience with any kind of planned economy had been in the period of War Communism; in the early 1930's, Russia, in his view, was engaged in a similar military mobilization and an equally harsh political struggle. For Stalin, such a crisis required sacrifices and justified extraordinary measures. Industrialization was a matter of human effort and determination, not a scholarly calculation of material resources. Industrialization meant big factories, breath-taking technical achievements, and construction projects of unparalleled magnitude, not limited, short-term investments, or funds squandered on agriculture, transport, and light industry that might better have

[5] For detailed analyses of the complex workings of the planning and industrial administrations, see the economic studies cited in the Bibliography for Chapters 4 and 5. The best short account of planning organization in the Stalin period can be found in Alexander Baykov's *The Development of the Soviet Economic System.*

been devoted to more tangible symbols of grandiose economic power. Stalin may not have wanted "a canal that could be seen from Mars" (Tvardovsky), but his obsession with economic monuments intensified as the industrialization drive progressed, thus injecting an increasingly irrational element into the planning process.

An early example of irrational construction—and one not peculiar to soviet Russia—was the ANT-20 passenger plane, developed during the Second Five Year Plan. This forty-two ton, eight-engined mechanical pterodactyl was one of several giant civilian and military aircraft built by the Soviet Union at that time (the famous engineer, Tupulov, designed a twelve-engined model which, however, never went aloft from the drawing board). The first ANT-20 lumbered around soviet air lanes on propaganda missions, consuming large quantities of gasoline, until it crashed. A second, six-engined version of this costly and impractical aircraft was built and flown for passenger traffic, but its fate is unknown.

Russia had hardly recovered from the war when the abortive scheme for changing the climate of Russia was inaugurated. This grandiose plan was to be fulfilled in two decades, during which millions of acres of steppe were to be protected from dry wind-storms and reclaimed through forestation, crop rotation, and irrigation from the five massive dams known as the "Great Stalin Constructions of Communism." Abandoned after his death, it was the crowning example during Stalin's last years of a gigantic waste of funds in the effort of soviet planners to build new and ever bigger pyramids.

Stalin's economic monuments, extravagant blunders that they were, never consumed very much of the total planned investment. They were, nevertheless, significant as the more bla-tant manifestations of a general disregard for resources and costs, both human and material, that was to result in serious problems for the soviet economy, particularly in the realm of agriculture, by the 1950's. The source for this irrationality in Stalinist planning was the plan directives, which were not necessarily governed by purely economic considerations, although these certainly played a large part in their formulation. The plan could only be as rational and efficient as its directives, although these were not the only factors determining its rationality and efficiency.

Rubber-stamped by the Central Committee of the soviet communist party, or by a party congress (when these were held), by the economic subcommittee of the Committee of Ministers (called the Economic Council after 1937), and later by the Supreme Soviet as well, the directives were passed onto the State Planning Commission (Gosplan). Gosplan was the highest planning agency in soviet Russia during Stalin's time. By the early 1930's, it had been expanded from what had been essentially an economic research institute performing occasional specific planning tasks to a large and powerful state agency, employing thousands of economists, statisticians, and other experts and overseeing the entire soviet economy through its forty-odd departments (1940).

The first task of Gosplan in any given year was to translate the annual party directives into a preliminary plan. This plan was highly tentative and generalized, and was based essentially on information which had been gathered through questionnaires and other research on current economic conditions and the performance of the previous plan. Gosplan also concerned itself, as annual planning progressed, usually during the last half of each year, with high-priority projects, the budget, trade, prices, and the maintenance of a reserve supply system, among other activities of lesser importance. The initial targets were passed down the line to subordinate planning and administrative agencies. At the bottom of this administrative pyramid, the individual factory formulated a precise plan in line with its new orders and forwarded this plan on the long journey back through supervisory agencies to the U.S.S.R. Gosplan. Such a procedure was not just one of calculation, but of bargaining as well. The efficiency and cohesion of the plan during these refinements was thus influenced by factors of a bureaucratic nature: the power and connections of agencies and officials, and other means of pressure that could be exerted to enhance particular interests, even if these conflicted with the aims and harmonious function of the plan as a whole.

At the next stage of the planning process, Gosplan was faced with the formidable task of coordinating the mass of information which it had received from below into a detailed allocation of resources and supplies for the entire economy. The end product of these calculations was known as material balances. The amount of factual knowledge and the grasp of the soviet economy that the material balances presupposed was stupendous and could not always be supplied. These difficulties were compounded by the neglect of economic analysis and computer technology in the Stalin era. Whether the more antiquated aspects of Marxist economics presented an impediment to sophisticated planning is questionable. As with the sciences, Marxism could be ignored when it got in the way, or used ritualistically without hindering the work at hand. However, the complex task of coordinating investments and supplies for interlocking chains of thousands of industries would have been substantially improved by the use of computational machinery and the development of sophisticated mathematical analysis. Instead, the balancing of resources and production was done by trial and error experimentation, and computation was made on the abacus. The result was a much higher level of miscalculation. Mistakes and bottlenecks could be dealt with only by the self-defeating expedients of sacrificing low-priority projects, downgrading consumer industries, or maintaining a costly reserve stockpile to meet emergencies. There is no evidence as to whether the new bureaucracy of "coordinate planning," built into Gosplan in 1935, provided remedies for these evils or intensified them.

The final version of the annual plan, after being linked to a technical plan (after 1941), and with the budget, prepared by the Ministry of Finance—with the tax and money structure—was approved by the appropriate higher spheres of the party and government. It was then put to work: delivery orders were made, authorizations were granted, contracts were signed.

The plan now became enmeshed in a vast managerial, requisitioning, and inspectional bureaucracy, with all the attendant evils of buraucratic government with which Russia had been familiar for centuries, as well as the costs involved in maintaining this elaborate machine. Almost at the beginning of the industrialization drive, a ministerial structure was created to execute the plan and administer the rapidly developing economy. Out of the three original Peoples Commissariats for economic affairs created in the early 1930's, there grew over thirty ministries by the death of Stalin. Many of these ministries became large conglomerations, which controlled not only thousands of factories comprehending entire industries or regions, but also sources of raw materials, supply industries, and distribution organizations. It was a kind of economic power both resembling and exceeding that of the great capitalistic monopolies of Western countries, but a form of organization modelled very largely along the lines of the old tsarist ministries (and using the same nomenclature): a directing Minister, advised by a Board or *kollegiya*, supervising subordinate agencies known as Main Administrations, which in turn were divided into Departments. Below these were individual factories or, occasionally, regional groupings of factories known as Trusts (a form and term carried over from the NEP period). Within the factory, the basic unit of production was the *tsekh*, or shop, yet another designation of distant tsarist times.

The Stalinist industrial ministries soon recapitulated the habits as well as the titles of tsarist bureaucracy. The tendency toward ministerial despotism and particularism, already observed in the administrative institutions of imperial Russia, came to characterize the larger industrial satrapies of the Soviet Union. As they accumulated power, they began to develop their own vested interests and momentums in policy making. Politically, this presented a challenge to other soviet power elites; economically, it meant disruption of the plan in both its formulative and implementative stages.

Within the structure of the Ministries and of Gosplan during most of the Stalin period, there also developed a large apparatus of procurement and disposal. Thousands of these supply offices were set up at various levels of industrial administration throughout the Soviet Union, certifying millions of requisitions. This created a complex system of authorization and a growing accumulation of red tape which not only obstructed industrial production, but, as in other large bureaucracies, gave rise to a parasitic class of expediters. The primary occupation of these "pushers" (*tolkachi*) was to hasten the process of supply, presumably through bribes, favors, and other shady forms of pressure. Russians referred to this ubiquitous underworld of connivance as *blat* (roughly, "pull" in American slang).

On the lower levels of the industrial bureaucracy, "fulfillment" of the plan was essentially a question of meeting quotas. The manager who fulfilled or exceeded his quota was rewarded; he who failed to do so was punished. The criterion for fulfillment was a quantitative one. This was the rule everywhere in Stalinist Russia—for the peasants on collective farms, and the slaves in prison camps, as well as for the Stakhanovites and the managers of large industrial enterprises. Such a primitive incentive system malfunctioned increasingly as the industrial economy became more and more complex. It led to numerous forms of deception, some of them strange and some familiar, most of them wasteful when not destructive. From juggling of accounts, to illicit stockpiling, to the production of inferior goods, among other devices for simulating or meeting higher production targets, these deceptions in turn bred a bureaucracy of inspection. This came ultimately to involve all the agencies of security, discipline, and control in communist Russia. The party, police, and trade unions inspected the factories as well as the ministries. State banks and tax collectors reviewed plant finances. *Tsunkhu*, the Central Administration of Economic Accounting (statistics) was used to keep Gosplan informed about industrial performance. Regular administrative control tightened as the ministerial apparatus burgeoned. A control bureaucracy was elaborated out of the old revolutionary workers and party inspection agencies. The new control centers required frequent progress reports from industrial management; yet a new army of inspectors and informants appeared in the factories. The soviet press worked diligently to expose corruption and inefficiency in industry; and public prosecutors investigated and punished wrongdoers. These multiple systems of surveillance, as might be expected, stimulated connivance on the part of local management and officials to hide discrepancies from the inspectors and to meet quotas. Inevitably, inspectors themselves were drawn into the web of corruption. It would be interesting, if difficult, to determine whether or not the enormous cost of policing soviet industrialization exceeded the waste which these measures saved.

One may conclude by observing that, as in tsarist days, the major defects of bureaucratic government became embedded in the soviet planning system: arbitrariness and delusion at the top, and corruption and deceit at the bottom. Because of the high degree of centralization, the neglect of technique, and over-bureaucratization, there was an improper flow of information and command from bottom to top and top to bottom, as well as improper coordination of the mass of information received. It was a viable way of industrialization and economic administration, but an expensive, wasteful, and inefficient one.

Stalin, like Peter the Great before him, was dependent in the last analysis on technology for the success of his industrialization program. The Stalinist method of industrialization was, by necessity and intention, autarkical. Communist Russia was still very much of an outcast; and it was preferable and possible for her to industrialize without slipping into dependence on Western capitalism and imperialism. Although such had been the cornerstone of the industrialization program of the tsarist ministers of finance, it was feasible for soviet Russia to develop free of these economic shackles by drawing from within for the necessary capital and resources, by the use of force to overcome backward social forces, and by the imposition of sacrifices on all groups of society. But no amount of taxing peasants and mobilizing workers would develop Russian technology. This could be done essentially in two ways: by training Russians and by using foreigners. However, both involved a costly dependence on the West.

Soviet policy during the industrialization drive was a recognition of these realities, if various devices of propaganda were used to extol the primacy and originality of communist and even tsarist technology. More substantive policy aimed to provide an adequate technological base for industrialization, and at the same time, to develop an independent soviet technology. This meant several very ambitious programs: the mobilization of existing Russian science and technology for the industrialization effort; the utilization of the Russian educational system, as well as of Western knowledge, to train a large number of new technicians and engineers, as required by the expanding economy; and the import of foreign experts to advise in the development of new industries and techniques wherever Russians could not do the job. Of all of Stalin's investments, this was probably the costliest and longest to come to fruition, but the most necessary. During most of the Stalinist industrialization drive, Russia remained heavily dependent on foreign technology.

The reorganization of Russian science and technology to serve industrialization can be seen first and foremost in the leading scientific institution of soviet Russia, the Academy of Sciences, although this reorientation extended along a much broader front, and ultimately came to embrace all scientific and technical schools down to the level of on-the-job training in factories. At the very beginning of the First Five Year Plan, in the tense months preceding the big collectivization push in 1929, the Academy of Sciences, relatively untouched by the government since the 1917 revolution, was shaken by a purge which lasted for more than a year. Although natural scientists were left untouched by the police, trusted communists and engineers were put in charge, and the work of the Academy was restricted largely to practical research which would contribute to the development of soviet industry. Academicians were ordered to elaborate their own plan, to be coordinated with the national plan.

Although the Academy of Sciences was harnessed in the service of the plan, its resources and activities were greatly expanded and at the same time consolidated. It became, in effect, a giant research laboratory for the industrialization drive. A similar reform was implemented in the nation's technical schools.

The plan demanded a vast new network of technical schools at all levels, if the requirements of the industrialization program were to be met. With the proclamation of Stalin's slogan, "Bolsheviks Must Master Technology," the growth of the technical education system was pursued with all the vigor of a Stakhanovite factory campaign. From 1928 to 1932, institutions of higher learning teaching technology and engineering almost quintupled, to 645 schools with 394,000 students. Lower technical schools of various levels also experienced significant growth, doubling in number and increasing their student population by 400 percent to almost one and three-quarter million. Many of the new technicians were women and many graduates of the new system were not properly trained. This was largely the result of undue emphasis on quantity (as in other areas of the soviet industrial system) at the expense of quality. A reform was instituted in 1935 which drastically eliminated unqualified students and schools and ended impractical democratic and pedagogical experimentation. The effectiveness of this reform, however, was vitiated by the turmoil of the purges and the war. It was not until after the Second World War that soviet technical education was able to achieve maturity in terms of meeting the needs of industry and maintaining a relative independence from the West.

During most of the Stalinist industrialization drive, Russia, in one way or another, had to rely heavily on the technology of the West. Western knowledge, in the form of books and research, was assimilated on a large scale in the technical schools and institutes. The more dramatic methods of espionage and the enslavement of foreign scientists and technicians were probably of greater significance for military projects than for industrial technology. When it came to application on a large scale of new techniques, the building of new enterprises, or even the development of new industries, the time-honored practices of importing machinery (by means of purchase or wartime foreign aid), sending students to study abroad, or contracting with foreign technicians to come to do the job, served soviet Russia best. Although hundreds of soviet technicians were sent to America, and an even larger number to Germany in the late 1920's, the big flow of equipment and trained personnel moved in the other direction during the industrialization drive. Much machinery came from Germany, particularly during the First Five Year Plan, although industrial apparatus and armaments were also imported from Italy, Japan, England, Sweden, and the United States. The United States came to be venerated as the ultimate repository of advanced technique, and as many as 5,000 American engineers have been estimated to have been employed by the soviet government during the 1930's. Some of this number were experienced engineers; others, politically sympathetic skilled workers who had immigrated to Russia. The Great Depression played a role in providing a larger and cheaper supply of both skilled foreign labor and more highly trained technicians from abroad. The soviet government, for its part, made no secret of the many large American firms that had contracted to build factories, dams, shipyards, refineries, roads, apartment houses, and even new cities in Russia. Ford, General Electric, Sperry, and RCA are among the more prominent American concerns in a list of twenty-five appended to the English edition of the First Five Year Plan. These contracts enabled the Russians to obtain the most advanced industrial technology in the world at a highly perfected stage of performance, without having to pay the tremendous costs of experimentation and development. It was not always as simple or inexpensive for Russian workmen to operate and maintain this complex machinery.

ECONOMIC GROWTH

Historical analysis of the soviet industrialization drive in the 1930's and 1940's points to the conclusion that it was a wasteful and exploitative method of promoting rapid economic growth. In this, it resembled the earlier industrial revolutions of Western countries. The kinds of injustice and malfunction were of a different order and intensity than those of capitalism, although they were not new to Russia. However, the fullest verification of these conclusions, and the final appraisal of the Stalinist method of industrialization cannot be rendered without a relatively precise statistical calculation of what was achieved, as well as of the costs involved.

Such a calculation has been one of the most difficult problems facing Western students of the soviet economy, because at the very beginning of the industrialization drive and for the next quarter of a century thereafter, a pall of secrecy and camouflage descended over most statistics. Some statistics were outrightly falsified, some more subtly obscured in vague terminology, some were omitted, and some counted twice. Some vital figures may not have been gathered, particularly during the purge years when statistical agencies fell into disfavor; other figures were wrong, not because of deliberate falsification for propaganda purposes, but as a result of the tendency toward exaggeration and deceit which manifested itself particularly in the lower levels of the soviet industrial bureaucracy. Inevitably, the sheer bulk of information, hastily gathered by a far-reaching network of statistical agencies (which employed a force of 2.3 million by the time of Stalin's death) became unwieldy, and errors were generated under the mounting weight of paper.

Few statistics were published in the Stalin era, although statistical analysis as a scientific discipline had obtained a recognizable degree of sophistication in Russia during the NEP period. Stalin appears to have been as suspicious of statisticians as he was of economists. Nor did statistics have the unqualified blessing of Marxist theory. Consequently, during the industrialization drive, it happened that the main function of statistics, like many a sister science, was to serve rather than to determine, to deceive and not to guide. However, self-deception was practiced as well as the hoodwinking of others; statisticians who published unfavorable figures were purged. All other material released for world consumption was grossly exaggerated, or so fragmentary as to be of little use.

This led scholars outside of the Soviet Union to challenge the veracity of official statistics. It was believed that soviet planners were guided by a separate set of secret, unfalsified statistics; but it was also reasoned that some of these relatively accurate figures found their way into the published materials. This was likely to occur when such figures coincided with the propaganda of soviet economic progress, or when they could be used to strengthen the credibility of other more fantastic and undemonstrable statistical claims.

European and American economists, particularly after the death of Stalin when more official figures became available, produced a substantial literature on the verification of soviet statistics. This critical apparatus, as well as the undeniable presence in the postwar period of a new and vast soviet economic power, stimulated an equally extensive scholarship which attempted to measure, as accurately as possible, the real industrial growth of the Soviet Union during the Stalin era. This research involved very complex problems, not only of sifting out of the mass of official data reliable series of figures upon which broader generalizations could be made, but also, in even greater statistical darkness as it were, of attempting to perceive the outlines of the burgeoning soviet military economy. Wartime industrial conversion and destruction, postwar reconstruction, and territorial losses and gains were all crucial factors which any credible approximation of soviet economic development in the hectic 1930's and 1940's had to take into account. To further complicate calculations there was the development of a new national industrial composition, and the difficulties and distortions involved in comparing it with preceding forms. Finally, the measuring rod of an index year which would not overly distort the changing values of goods and prices over a span of a quarter of a century had to be selected.

A number of highly involved calculations have been made in recent years to answer such questions. These estimates are based on various groups of statistics; they survey specific or broader areas of the soviet economy, and utilize one or more different indexes. In a general historical essay such as this, it will not be appropriate to review or attempt to evaluate the sophisticated methodologies involved, but rather, to point out the main areas of consensus.[6] Most estimates utilize indexes for

[6] See the bibliography for Chapter 4 for the various detailed studies which were undertaken.

earlier rather than more recent times. This is done to avoid minimizing soviet achievements: index figures based on later years, it has generally been concluded, tend to do this. Thus, particularly since many computations go back to the beginning of the Stalin industrialization drive, error would seem to be, if anywhere, on the side of exaggeration. Nevertheless, of seven prominent indexes of soviet industrialization published in the West in the past eighteen years, all are substantially lower than official soviet figures. The highest of these estimates (Seton) gives 390, 463, 717, and 1116 for the years 1937, 1940, 1950, and 1955 (1928 equals 100). Seton's figures range from roughly two thirds to seven eights of the soviet ones for the same years (these are: 445, 503, 1009, and 1866). Although the range of difference between the Western estimates is often greater than the difference between them and the soviet figures, there is an area of relative consensus among the five more begrudging computations (Nutter, Shimkin–Leedy, Kaplan–Moorsteen, Jasny, and Clark, the latter two not carrying their estimations into the later years). These five show much less variance among each other than the gaps among higher estimates and soviet ones. When they are averaged, we arrive at the figures 275, 283, 426, and 621 for the years measured. In other words, most of the Western economists whom we have cited commenting on the growth of soviet industry during the Stalin period would see it as having expanded almost three times after the first ten years, four times after the second decade, and six times by the mid-1950's. During the same period, soviet figures envisage an expansion of six, ten, and just over eighteen times. The consensus of most Western estimates thus ranges roughly between one third and one half of the soviet claim for the achievements of the Stalinist industrialization drive.

Estimates of the annual growth rate follow a similar pattern. Soviet statisticians claim an average rate of 11.9 percent yearly from 1928 to 1955. Some Western economists would see about 6.9 percent for that period, and for the early years of the industrialization drive (1928–1940), 9.9 percent (Nutter). This was a high rate of growth compared to many capitalist economies at a comparable phase of development, although not dramatically higher than the tsarist industrial boom of the 1890's (8.03 percent), and much lower than the pace of the NEP period (27.7 percent, 1922–1927). Both the tsarist and the NEP industrializations, of course, started from a much smaller base, the latter from an industrial ruin producing a mere 13 percent of the prewar level (see Chapter 3). The overall growth rate for the soviet period, 1917–1955, was about equal to that of the last half century of tsarist rule, 1860–1917, approximately five percent (allowing for the drastic decline of industrial production in both world wars and under the respective regimes).

The tsarist industrial system was severely strained by the First World War. Similarly, the Stalinist industrialization drive was profoundly inhibited by several years of total and highly destructive warfare. However, apart from this period of exceptional hardship, soviet economic growth in peacetime years did not follow a uniform and sharp upward curve concurring with the chronology of the five year plans. Periods of growth alternated with serious slowdowns in industrial production. Western economists (Jasny, Zaleski) have identified two such slumps in the 1930's. Similar downswings of a lesser magnitude have been observed in the 1920's (see Chapter 3) and in the post-Stalin period. These fluctuations can not be equated with the cyclical crises characteristic of capitalist economies. Although of a comparable severity, the causes and effects are different. Economic and administrative factors—defects of the planning system discussed earlier—played an important role; but even more decisive were forces which were essentially political in nature. As a highly disruptive social revolution involving the massive application of force and consequent widespread dislocation in the Russian countryside and cities, collectivization figures largely in the background of the nearly disastrous economic crisis which reached rock bottom in the winter of 1932–1933. Another major slowdown, although less severe than its predecessor, was clearly in evidence after 1937 and lasted until 1940. This slump can not be disassociated from the purges, although some economists would see growth cycles also attributable to the purges in numerous industries during the mid-1930's, a period of relative overall prosperity. To attempt to understand these fluctuations, it will be helpful to examine the phases of soviet economic development during the Stalin era in greater detail and in chronological order.

In the early 1930's, the soviet economy not only failed to achieve the largely propagandistic goals of the First Five Year Plan, as one would expect, but could not maintain ascending rates of growth, even in specially favored sectors of the economy, such as heavy industry, into which most investment had been diverted. The growth rate for large-scale industry as a whole declined from 20 percent in 1928 to 5.2 percent in 1932.[7] The drop in the main extractive, metallurgical, and machine industries followed a similar course. If one brings into this figure the decline of lumbering and small-scale industry (the latter was almost wiped out in the same period), a rate of only 4 percent for 1932 is attained. Total steel production barely increased at all during the same years, inching up from 5.8 million tons in 1929 to 5.9 million tons in 1932. There was a decline in the actual output of most heavy industries, except construction and electric power, as seen in figures for January of 1932 as compared to those for the same month a year later.

The decline in agriculture and the consumer economy was far more severe during the First Five Year Plan. Gross farm output went down 20 percent. Dairy production included in this figure fell into an even more drastic decline. Production in the main textile industries either rose insignificantly (cotton), or actually declined (linen and worsteds). Similarly, consumer foodstuffs, like sugar, or durables, like roofing iron, were drastically curtailed from 1928 to 1933. The construction of private housing practically ceased, and the proportion of investment in public housing dropped to just over half of the rate of the NEP period. As we have seen, real wages were halved, as was the consumption of meat. Bread consumption followed the decline

[7] Most figures for the 1932–1933 slump are derived from Jasny, *Soviet Industrialization 1928–1952,* who has given the fullest analysis of the fluctuations of the Soviet economy.

in grain production—10 percent. While the birth rate dropped approximately a third during the First Five Year Plan and untold millions starved to death, population growth in 1933 has been hypothesized to have declined by over 97 percent from the figure of five years before, from two and one half million a year in the late 1920's to only 74,000 from 1932 to 1933.[8]

Much of this economic disaster, although not its most gruesome consequences, as we have seen earlier in the chapter, was planned: the drastic contraction of the consumer economy, the vastly increased taxation of agriculture, even if overall agricultural production declined, to say nothing of a crop failure. The vast expansion of the heavy industrial base that was undertaken would naturally produce a lower figure for the rate of development. Allowing for this, the volume (as well as the quality) of industrial production had fallen by 1933 to a level far below what could be defined as substantial and rapid economic growth. As in 1929, so only four years later the soviet economy had reached an impasse. Although of a different type, the troubles stemmed ultimately, as so often before in Russian history, from the agricultural sector.

The fundamental cause of the crisis of 1933 was collectivization. The immense pressures of forced reorganization of agriculture had not only disrupted production in the countryside; it also had profoundly inhibiting effects on Russian industry. Millions of peasants flooded into the cities, an unskilled and unreliable labor force which the new Russian industries were not prepared to absorb or train. What emerged was a bloated and largely untutored proletariat, dazed industrial nomads incessantly migrating from factory to factory or back to the land. The result was a notable decline of labor productivity.

The miscalculations and obsessions characteristic of the planning system, particularly in this very early stage of its development, also played an important role in slowing down the pace of industrialization during the First Five Year Plan. As has

[8] Lorimer. See Bibliography.

been indicated at length earlier in this chapter, a disproportionate amount of investment was pumped into heavy industry. Much
was squandered on gigantic projects, which would not become
productive for extended periods of time. At the same time,
steps had not been taken to develop technology and a transportation system adequate to meet the needs of the new industrial
complex. The result was inefficiency, waste, and costly dependence on foreign engineers, whose notable achievements
were never, however, adequate to the demand. The building up
of tremendous transportation bottlenecks was largely the result
of a decision to gamble on the capacity of the existing railroad
system to absorb, with only minimum investment in new construction, the freight demands of rapidly growing industrial
combinations and regions. The gamble was lost: by 1932, back-
logs of several millions of tons of freight, particularly bulky
materials, such as fuels, grain, iron, and lumber, had clogged the
soviet railway system. Despite the completion of a few significant high priority lines (the Turkistan-Siberian and Urals-
Kuznets), it was clear by 1933 that only a massive investment in
the improvement and enlargement of the soviet railway network as a whole would avert a transportation breakdown.

That the soviet economy had reached a crisis by this time,
in technology, agriculture, and industry as well as in transportation, is evidenced by the major policy changes which came in
1934 and 1935. The new policies did not represent either a "retreat" or a "liberalization" (this was the beginning of the purge
era), but rather, an attempt to achieve greater efficiency and
incentive, while maintaining the existing pace of development
for heavy industry. The push toward greater efficiency and incentive was expressed in a number of policies, some of which
have been outlined in previous sections of this book. The Stakhanovite movement and the overhaul of the technical schools in
1935 and 1936 were notable attempts to improve standards and
quality. At the same time, the railway system underwent a
transformation. Investment in the railways was vastly increased;
and Lazar Kaganovich, the "black tornado," perhaps Stalin's best

and toughest administrator, was placed in charge of reforming organization and procedure. This task was accomplished with unusual success in a very short time. Planning became more realistic and balanced; not only were the railroads provided with necessary funds, but investments in consumer industry and public housing were substantially increased. Investments in heavy industry were maintained, at a time when big projects initiated during the First Five Year Plan were beginning to pay off. Although the low rate of investment in agriculture also remained constant, violence was receding in the countryside, and the peasants were conceded ownership of livestock and small private plots, the produce of which could be sold on free markets in the cities. Pressure was also relaxed on the urban worker and consumer. Wages improved, some new housing was built, and rationing was ended. The end of these restrictions was preceded by increased investment in light industry, and a minimal availability of consumer goods.

The result of the new policies was very substantial economic growth in the mid-1930's. The new industrial economy took form. This meant not only a new composition of the nation's industries in which war and heavy industry (in contrast to the tsarist industrial pattern) predominated over consumer industry, while small industry largely disappeared; it signified a new disposition of industry into hitherto underdeveloped parts of the Soviet Union.

By 1937, the production of iron, steel, and other ferrous metals had quadrupled the levels of a decade before, as did the output of fuels, electric power, and chemical products (although the latter began from a much smaller base and remained feebly developed for some time to come). There was a vast increase in the production of machinery during the period of the Second Five Year Plan, about 1800 percent over the NEP level. In absolute terms for selected industries for which we have substantial figures,[9] this growth can be seen in the following table:

[9] Figures in this paragraph and table are derived largely from the Appendices in Nutter (see Bibliography).

	1913	1927/28	1937
Steel (rolled, ingots, castings)	7,891,000 MT	——	30,700,000
Pig iron	4,216,000 "	——	14,490,000
Crude oil	9,230,000 "	——	28,500,000
Coal	33,120,000 "	——	147,970,000
Chemicals (several types)	584,590 "	——	8,818,760
Tractors	——	1,270	50,980
Automobiles	——	100	18,200
Steam and gas turbines	——	35,700 kw.	1,068,000

The total value of soviet industrial production in 1937 has been estimated at 150 billion rubles (current prices, deducting the turnover tax).[10]

The most spectacular growth within the heavy industrial sector of the soviet economy during the mid-1930's can be seen in the transportation system. Little was done in the area of civilian and commercial air transport and even less for road construction, paving or the manufacture of automobiles, although a more significant number of trucks and buses were being produced by 1937, mainly for use within the cities. In its main emphases, soviet transportation policy followed the tsarist tradition. This meant rivers, canals, and railroads. The Volga continued to serve as the main channel for inland marine commerce, as it had for a millennium, its value enhanced by the completion in 1937 of a canal link with Moscow. The White Sea-Baltic canal, opened in 1933, provided a vital connection between the newly developing northern regions and the renovated tsarist canal systems of northwestern Russia. In the south, the development of several winter-summer ports on the Black Sea made this sea the artery for almost all of Russia's foreign trade.

Although during the 1930's Russia's inland waterways carried a substantially increased volume of freight, they carried only

[10] Jasny.

a tiny fraction of the total. The main task of transporting goods and materials was given to the railroads, which were allotted about 40 percent additional investment funds in 1934 and 1935. This however did not mean the construction of new lines as the answer to the bottlenecks of the First Five Year Plan. Until the period immediately prior to World War II, when line construction was accelerated, total rail mileage did not greatly exceed what it had been just prior to the fall of the tsarist regime, about 50,000 miles. However, a major effort was made in the mid-1930's to improve existing facilities and increase capacities with more and heavier track on the main trunk lines connecting the old industrial regions of European Russia, additional equipment, new designs, more efficient techniques for loading and dispatching, and better on-the-job performance. The result was a remarkable increase in capacity and in the volume of freight carried. By 1940, this amounted to 415 billion metric tons, more than two and one half times the 1932 volume. The growth of soviet railroads followed a steady upward course after 1934, except for a drop in 1937, largely attributable to a temporary but drastic cut in investment, to inefficiency arising from changes in managerial personnel, and perhaps to the intrusion of the purges into all levels of organization.

Consumer industries, which had stagnated considerably during the First Five Year Plan, resumed during the mid-1930's the growth that had been characteristic of them since the late tsarist period, although modestly. This can be seen in the table on the following page of selected textile, housing, and food industries.[11]

This moderate revival of consumer industry was reflected both in the figures for the apportionment of investment in the mid-1930's and those for increases in per capita consumption and real income.[12] Investment in light industry increased about 50 percent to 2,376,000 rubles, while heavy industry remained at its former level of investment (except for transport). Housing investment also went up by about a third, and agriculture, a fifth. Nevertheless, the total investment in housing and light industry

[11] Figures derived from the tables in Nutter.
[12] Consumption and investment figures from Jasny.

	1913	1927/28	1933	1937
Cotton yarn	271,000 MT	324,000	367,300	532,900
Linen yarn	53,300 "	61,600	57,600	97,500
Woolen yarn	46,500 "	49,500	67,500	76,600
Cotton fabrics	2,582,000,000 m	2,678,000,000	2,732,000,000	3,448,000,000
Linen fabrics	120,000,000 "	174,400,000	140,500,000	285,200,000
Woolen fabrics (incl. worsteds)	105,000,000 "	117,000,000	86,100,000	108,300,000
Roofing iron	406,200 MT	369,300	102,900	179,000
Refined sugar	828,000 "	656,000	349,000	1,032,000
Vodka	178,900,000 dkl	55,500,000	—	89,700,000
Cigarettes	22,100,000,000 "	49,500,000,000	62,700,000,000	89,200,000,000
Cheap tobacco (*Makhorka*)	3,934,000 20-kg crates	4,293,000	2,513,000	5,343,000

in 1937 equalled approximately one third of the total investment in heavy industry and transportation (16,646,000,000 rubles). Urban per capita food consumption rose moderately from the austerity levels of 1933. There was a slight rise in the consumption of meat and dairy products and a more substantial increase in the purchase of bread and potatoes. But by 1937, these levels still remained far below those of 1928, about 60 percent, as did real per capita income, which Jasny estimates for peasants and workers alike in 1936 at three fifths of that of 1928. Population, of course, began to increase and to approach the rates which preceded the collectivization years. Not unrelated to this was a substantial increase of expenditures in the mid-1930's on health, education, and other social benefits.

It was obvious that, despite the continuing and drastic restriction of consumption and agriculture, a new economic dynamism was emerging in the mid-1930's, which was generating wealth at a greater rate. It was now possible to permit the diversion of substantial investment into bottlenecked or neglected areas of the economy, and to ease somewhat the burden on the people themselves. Significant as both cause and effect in this accelerated growth was the emergence of a new soviet industrial composition. Tsarist industry had developed mainly in the ports and cities and surrounding districts of European Russia and the old imperial western borderlands—Moscow, St. Petersburg, Riga, Vilna, and Odessa, among others (see Chapters 1 and 2). Except for the Donbas-Krivoi Rog metallurgical complex, the disposition of tsarist industry had not been determined by rational calculations of the proximity of resources, fuels, means of transport, and markets, but rather, was an expression of the commercial, political, and even religious structure of preindustrial Russia. The railroads connected the grain fields and ports; St. Petersburg, as the center of government and a leading port, became a commercial, industrial and financial hub strongly linked to the West; the Old Believers were important to the development of the Moscow textile industry.

The planned industrial distribution which took shape in the mid-1930's was designed to organize and locate new industries on sound economic as well as strategic foundations, while at the same time continuing the development of the older industrial centers. This involved the construction, characteristic of soviet planning, of large industrial combinations linked to fuel supplies, raw materials, and markets by enlarged railway lines. The aim was to consolidate as far as possible all phases of production and supply in one area, utilizing large factory units for purposes of economizing. Thus, although most investment was poured into the expansion of the older Ukrainian and Moscow centers, a vast new industrial complex was built in the Urals. Russia's first important metallurgical center, built by Peter the Great over iron deposits that were still rich after a century of exploitation and a longer succeeding period of decay, was rebuilt on a far grander scale, but for different reasons than those which motivated the first industrializing tsar. The Urals were too far from Western Europe to be in great danger of destruction or capture by an invading army; but they were close enough to Siberian coal fields to be assured of an adequate fuel supply carried by modern railroads. The Urals-Kuznetsk complex was the result. While older Urals industrial centers, such as Nizhne-Tagil were rebuilt, Magnitogorsk, a whole new city of steel, machine, and armaments factories, arose out of the countryside in the 1930's. The rich coal deposits of Kuznetsk were also capable of supplying other new industrial combinations in the Urals and Siberia. The east, however (Siberia as well as Central Asia), although earmarked for a relocation of Russian industry, was not in fact substantially developed until the Second World War.

Beginning in 1937, the tempo of soviet industrialization began once again to slacken. The increase of gross industrial output during this period has been estimated at about 10 percent (exclusive of 1939 territorial acquisitions), contrasted to the 70 percent growth of the years 1934–1936. Although this near standstill was not as severe as the slump of 1932–1933, it was of longer duration. A real upswing did not make itself apparent until 1940. As with the First Five Year Plan, stagnation during the Third Five Year Plan was pronounced in the very sector of the economy favored by large investments, heavy industry. Consumer industries, transport, and agriculture, which were largely deprived of resources, suffered as they had during the collectivization period. However, in contrast to the early 1930's, the factory worker's position improved.

There is little doubt that the purges and war preparations, the two reasons most frequently given for the soviet industrial slump of the late 1930's, played an important role in disrupting the growth pattern established in the immediately preceding years. But these two factors cannot be said to provide the complete explanation of the fluctuations of this complex period, which still remain to be fully clarified. It must be remembered that large-scale purges began in the mid-1930's and diminished in their intensity and scope after 1938. Extensive war preparation also began much earlier, in 1934, and slackened to some extent during the period of the Nazi-Soviet pact. The build-up of the Red Army, however, came in the late 1930's, although this probably had less impact on industry than on the villages.

Some features of soviet economic growth and stagnation in the late 1930's are more open to a reasonable and clear explanation. Certain industries, high on the list of war mobilization priorities, maintained high rates of growth. The production of armaments doubled in the late 1930's, which was in part the result of a strenuous military build-up begun four years earlier. Throughout the Second and Third Five Year Plans, there was heavy investment in the new and strategically essential nonferrous metals industries of Central Asia. Electric power, in which there had been substantial investment and progress since the time of Lenin, and coal production, well advanced with the opening of the Kuznetsk basin, could be expected to forge ahead without outside stimulation, as they did.

By 1937, the clear soviet policy pattern had been established that, when it was deemed necessary to divert resources elsewhere, the first areas of the economy called upon to sacrifice would be consumer industries and agriculture (with transportation next in line as an expendable item, or at least, as a sector capable of producing at high levels under conditions of deprivation and neglect for limited periods of time). The reallocation of investment and taxation for the continuing benefit of heavy industry was repeated in the late 1930's, but funds were also allocated for the extensive build-up of the war machine. While investments in armaments went up 30 percent a year, those in consumer industries dropped 15 percent. Investment in railways was cut back drastically in 1937, although temporarily, after the distressing consequence of a 75 percent drop in the volume of freight carried. Under the shadow of war, extensive railroad line construction was resumed. The relative well-being of soviet agriculture by 1937, not only in terms of grain production and procurement, but also in the marked increase in per capita real income of peasants, may have been the signal for a cut back in 1938 and 1939. This involved not only investment in agriculture, but also the allotments of livestock and private gardens conceded to the peasantry in the mid-1930's. At the same time, delivery quotas were raised.

Despite this diversion of resources into the heavy industry sector, there was a slowdown in the production of some essential nonmilitary goods, and actual decline in the output of others. While steel production increased by only 200,000 tons from 1938 to 1940 (just over 1 percent), there was a slackening in oil production and a drop in chemicals and machinery production. The purges provide one key to this failure to effectively utilize investment. One probable consequence of the purges was timid or sycophantic planning (multiplication of grandiose projects). The purges swept Gosplan as well as the rest of the Soviet economic bureaucracy. However, a more enduring disruption in this violent period, and one which may explain the decline in production after the purges began to abate in 1938, was the detainment and total waste of thousands of high ranking industrial executives in prisons or at forced manual labor. Many of these men were replaced by inexperienced people, sometimes by students fresh out of school, whose mistakes may have depressed soviet industry for a considerable time after the diminution of terror. On the other hand, the purge era was a time of relative security for rank and file labor. Both real and money wages went up, a privileged elite of Stakhanovites, beholden and loyal to the regime, was being built up, and labor discipline for the others, although austere, was a long way from its war-time severity. If the government, for political reasons, adopted a policy of relaxation of pressure on workers, this policy did not have the added benefit of increasing individual output. It was a "Time of Troubles," and, as in previous periods of such disturbances in Russian and soviet history, the people once again began to migrate in large numbers. The labor restrictions of 1940 put an end to this nomadism, and the resultant increase in labor productivity is seen as one of the factors in the industrial upswing beginning in that year.

If the 1930's were the iron age of soviet industrialization, the Second World War was its heroic period. No less monumental in its proportions than the industrialization push of the early five year plans was the massive conversion and relocation of soviet industry in the face of the German invasion. As armies mobilized, a much more rigid discipline of factory and farm labor was introduced. Rationing was again imposed upon the consumer. Consumer industries were cut to the bone; and most heavy industries were rapidly converted to the production of munitions, armaments, and military machinery. As the Germans advanced and the Russian armies began to collapse, entire sections of industries were dismantled, moved, and reassembled in the Asian interior. According to soviet figures, 1360 factories, most of them very large, were carried by hundreds of thousands of railroad freight cars and trucks to the Urals, Western Siberia, Central Asia and the lower Volga region. A third of Russia's factory workers went with them. Such a powerful influx of man-power and equipment accelerated the development of these eastern industrial centers. By the end of the war, the Urals had surpassed the Ukraine in iron, steel, and armaments production; and important metallurgical and fuel industries had been firmly rooted in Central Asia and Siberia.

It would appear—and was predicted—that the soviet rail-way system, already taxed to the utmost by the peacetime industrialization effort, would collapse under the strain of war. Although the Germans seized 40 percent of the rail lines at the very beginning of hostilities, most of the locomotives and rolling stock escaped to the East, where it was possible, with rigorous curtailment of nonessential travel and shipments, for this enlarged fleet to absorb the pressure of increased military traffic. As elsewhere, Lend Lease supplies and the extensive employment of female labor relieved critical shortages of machinery and manpower.

While a new industrial Russia grew in the East, the Western republics, which for four years became battlefields or occupied territory, were subjected to unparalleled devastation. Industrial rock bottom was reached by the end of 1941, when production losses through occupation or relocation brought total production to half its preinvasion level. Grain losses were even greater. Recovery was substantial and rapid, as eastern industry was built up and the tide of war changed. Foreign aid made up for at least half of what had been lost; territorial gains, which were extensive by 1945, accounted for about a tenth.[13] Reparations, confiscations, booty, and other forms of levy imposed upon eastern European countries and the prolonged corvée of Axis prisoners of war accounted for perhaps another 10 percent. But no substitute forms of labor could adequately replace the millions of able-bodied men who were killed and the millions more that would not be born. Accurate figures are still not available; one guess[14] as to the total number of military and civilian casualties (including prisoners, millions of whom died) is 14,300,000. The obliteration of several millions of civilian and industrial structures, to which must be added the loss of large quantities of machinery and livestock, necessitated an immense reconstruction effort. Thus, postwar recovery and reconversion in the Soviet Union was slower than in other of the Allied countries, none of whom had suffered as grievously. For Russian industry, it lasted at least three years; for other less favored sectors of the economy, the full restoration of prewar conditions and capacities came much later. Until 1951, investment, production, and income in the consumer and agricultural economies were below the prewar

13 Nutter's estimate.
14 Lorimer.

level. The depression of agriculture and peasant income lasted until Stalin's death. Transportation, which also made its recovery by 1948, fell into a new slump, which persisted until 1954.

During the last years of the 1940's and the beginning 1950's, the growth of heavy industry accelerated at a very high rate: by 1950, industrial production had exceeded the 1940 level by 40 percent. The main factors that account for this prosperity are that soviet heavy industry not only continued to benefit from massive infusions of investment, but was still in a process of recovery and the attainment of full use of capacities. These factors also help to explain the economic slowdown which characterizes the last two years of Stalin's rule. Transportation and agriculture, particularly the latter, were severely depressed, and were dragging down the economy as a whole. Although the base was broader, and output was increasing substantially, the growth rates for the principal heavy industries were much lower than those of the mid-1930's. Food and textile industries were doing better than in the 30's; but the production of consumer durables was growing much more slowly than before.

The military build-up, greatly intensified in the Korean War period, is the main reason for the sluggishness of the late Stalinist economy, although such preparations were not as depressing as those of the late 1930's. Other operative factors were inherent in the Stalinist mode of industrialization, and repeated the patterns of the early five year plans. Foremost was the continuing lack of necessary investment in agriculture, the heavy taxation of the peasantry and the continuing attack on their private economy. Despite some growth of consumer industries, consumption remained strangled in a net of high prices and low wages. Planning remained erratic and imprecise: the continuing mania for gigantic, long-term projects was accompanied by a widespread reluctance to disrupt production schedules with new technology. Investments and innovations in the transportation system, such as oil pipelines, were long overdue. The slave camps were proving themselves wasteful and difficult to manage. Industrial administration was colorless and timid.

On March 5, 1953, the Stalinist industrialization drive, the harshest and most dynamic phase of the industrialization of Russia, came to an end with the death of the man who had been largely responsible for it. Stalin died the ruler of a powerful, industrialized state, but one which, although not stagnant, was losing momentum and was beset with serious problems. He also died rigidly persevering in the industrialization methods which had been developed in the 1930's. But the "iron age" of soviet industrialization was passing; and the system which had evolved in this period of violence and rapid change was no longer appropriate for the more stable environment of an advanced industrial economy. Essential human and material resources had been exploited and strained too long and too harshly. They were no longer able to carry the burden of crash industrialization. The horse of soviet agriculture, particularly, could no longer jump the high fence of heavy industry (to use Khrushchev's image). Industrial growth would continue at a rapid pace after Stalin. So substantial was the productive increase in the 1950's that it can (and has been) argued that soviet industrialization really begins in earnest in the postwar period. This, of course, is a purely quantitative statement. The system was created under Stalin; and after him, no new system would be introduced. Although new policies would be devised and implemented, their purpose would be, not the revolutionary social and economic change characteristic of the Stalin era, but rather, the rationalization of the existing system and the resolution of new complexities which it was creating.

5 / Industrialized Russia

THE POST–STALIN REFORMS, 1953–1970

The history of Russia in the generation after 1725 was captured brilliantly by Sir Bernard Pares in just one phrase: "Peter's new Russia without Peter." So the character of the soviet industrialized economy in the sixteen years following the passing of Stalin could aptly be summarized: "Stalin's new Russia without Stalin," As in the post-Petrine period, the new system remained intact, operated by many of the same men who had served its creator. In the 1950's and 1960's, as in the 1730's and 1740's, it was not permitted to lapse, because the industrial war machine that had been built was essential for the maintenance of Russia's security and position as a newly emerged great power. Palace revolutions rippled the surface of things, in the eighteenth century as in the twentieth, while underneath, the economic structure quietly expanded and the new state and society established itself. The successors of Stalin, like those of Peter, were the pupils of their master. They possessed neither his capacity for cruelty, nor his power to change history. He became both a tyrant to disown and a model to emulate. The post-Stalin period, like the post-Petrine era, was thus one of continuity, but also one of modification and innovations.

The first economic reforms, which came almost immediately after the death of Stalin, were aimed at modification. There was a move to eliminate the obvious excesses of his industrialization policies. This reform is identified with Georgii M. Malenkov, a protégé of Kaganovich and Stalin, whose faction had established a temporary primacy in the struggle for power that characterized soviet political life during the mid-1950's. The first concessions were made to the Russian consumer, barely a few weeks after Stalin's death. Prices on foodstuffs, clothing, and other consumer goods were cut, although not drastically. This was followed by a moderate expansion of some consumer industries. The taxpayer came next and was treated in similar fashion. Mandatory bond purchases, which had long functioned as a form of taxation, were reduced, netting the wage earner a few extra rubles of take-home pay. Political prisoners and peasants also became beneficiaries of the new policy. Many of the former were included in a 1953 amnesty which marked the beginning of the breakup of the Stalinist labor camp empire, long seen as an economic liability. The move was made to increase peasant income, incentive, and productivity through price hikes, the reduction of quotas and taxes, and, as in the 1930's, there was an extension of the peasant's right to maintain livestock and produce foodstuffs on his own plot of land for sale in private markets. But the *kolkhozniki* were also pressured into putting in more time working for the Collective, a large portion of the profits of which were still taxed away by the state. The more fantastic of Stalin's projects were dropped by Malenkov, although the disproportionate emphasis on heavy industry was continued. The end of the Korean war brought a curtailment of the military expenditure that had worked to depress the economy in Stalin's last years, but work on nuclear bombs went on. The Stalinist trend toward top-heavy bureaucracy continued unabated.

The policies of the Malenkov era were not a significant departure from the Stalinist system, but were essentially a gesture, and one with political overtones, an indication that the worst elements of Stalinism would be renounced by the then dominant party faction. Even the notorious Beria, still head of the secret police, loudly advocated these liberal policies to gain support. The fact that the actual changes were minimal, beyond a token increase in the output of consumer goods, was reflected in the economic situation of the Malenkov era, 1953–1955. The reduction in military expenditure helped to raise industrial production substantially by 1954, but agriculture deteriorated steadily during the same period, and it was obvious that the minor concessions made to the peasantry after Stalin's death were not compensating for a quarter of a century of neglect. By 1955, Malenkov's political enemies, led by Khrushchev, had gained strength sufficient to oust him. The economic grounds for his removal were Stalinist ones—weakening of heavy industry and endangering war preparations by reckless investment in consumer industry—although Malenkov's real failure was in agriculture. His policy toward the consumer was continued by his successors: the big reforms came in agriculture.

Nikita S. Khrushchev was, like Malenkov, a high-ranking member of the Stalinist party apparatus, and also, like his predecessor, a specialist more in organizational matters than in economic problems. After defeating Malenkov, and soon after ousting the old-line Stalinists who had been his allies against Malenkov, Khrushchev appropriated as his own, and with much greater vigor, the "rightist" program of concessions to the consumer, wage earner, and peasant that he had previously so vigorously denounced. Khrushchev was an accomplished politician; he knew how to organize support within the party and he could sense which policies would attract support from the masses outside the apparatus. But Khrushchev was also of the school of Stalin; wary of economic expertise and suspicious of technocrats, he tended to place his reliance on expensive, risky crash programs and purely administrative solutions. But the days for such extravagance had passed. The failure of Khrushchev's grandiose economic projects helped to bring about his overthrow in 1964.

At the beginning, Khrushchev adhered to the Malenkovian policy of moderate concessions to the man in the street. But it was not in line with Khrushchev's flamboyant and earthy style to articulate his program in moderate tones; nor was this in keeping with the party politics of the time, characterized by intense factional struggle, in which initially rational economic policies could be distorted as they became involved in political maneuvres. Although Khrushchev adhered to these moderate policies to the very end of his public career, there were times, particularly when things were not going so well with the soviet economy, when he began to break earlier promises, to tighten up, and to reach out for more drastic remedies. But the beginnings were cautious. While Stalin was being denounced with vehemence and sarcasm in Khrushchev's historic speeches of 1956, more of the barbs of the Georgian dictator's system were being removed. Dismantlement of the slave system continued, although a smaller network of penal labor colonies and several forms of compulsory labor were retained. Wages of industrial workers were raised and systematized, the work week was shortened, and the draconic labor discipline of former times was softened. Obligatory purchases of bonds, which had been decreased under Malenkov, then raised again, were ended by Khrushchev. Although the redemption date of existing bond issues was postponed for another two decades, such manipulations had been performed so frequently under Stalin that most workers probably viewed the piles of government certificates in their drawers as so much paper, and thanked Khrushchev heartily for the extra money this reform gave them each payday. His vow to abolish income taxes was not, however, fulfilled. But pensions were substantially raised, and, following the Malenkov precedent in agriculture, peasant income was increased through higher prices and a relaxation of the system of compulsory deliveries.

In the field of planning and industrial administration, Khrushchev was far less flexible—or sensible, as he was later accused —from almost the beginning. He was as extravagant with military expenditures, including the costly space program, and with investments in long-term construction, as Stalin had been, until the exhaustion of capital forced him into cutting corners. Unlike Stalin, Khrushchev did not plunder the agricultural and consumer economies to pay other bills. The time had passed when such disproportions were tolerable, either politically or economically. Also departing from the Stalinist pattern, Khrushchev encouraged economic research and discussion; but he was hesitant to implement new programs based on the theories of his experts or to permit initiative in more than an experimental way. A product of the Stalin era, and a true child of Russian tradition, Khrushchev put his faith in administrative reform, inspection, and, as the economic situation deteriorated in the last years of his rule, in crash programs and panaceas.

The administrative reform of soviet industry in 1957 appears on the face of things to be one of the perennial reshufflings of bureaucratic agencies characteristic of Russian history, in which the main impulse has been either centralization or decentralization, the check of ministerial despotism, or the eradication of local vested interests. In Khrushchev's reform, as in earlier instances in tsarist and soviet history, political motives were as important as economic considerations. It has been suggested that Khrushchev wanted to strengthen his party following in Moscow at the expense of powerful interests in the state economic bureaucracy by shifting leading personnel to the provinces. At the same time, the gigantic industrial ministries built up in Stalin's time were obstructing the smooth functioning of the economy through the inevitable duplication of effort that such a highly centralized system promoted.

Khrushchev, all powerful by 1957, pushed his reform with vigor. Twenty-five ministries in Moscow were dismantled; and bureaucrats packed their bags for the trek to the provinces, where over a hundred territorial economic councils (*sovnarkhozy*) were set up, designed to cooperate with local authorities in more efficiently attending to the peculiar and the general economic problems of particular regions. The reform was short lived. Hardly had it been implemented than measures aimed at the centralization of the economy were being taken. As Stalin had so often done, Khrushchev found it convenient, in 1959, to introduce a new system of inspectional agencies—Party Control Commissions, which could keep a closer watch on factories and localities. Three years later, these agencies were expanded. It was in the same year of 1962 that a new wave of administative reforms swept away much of the regionalized industrial system created only five years before. The *sovnarkhozy* were consolidated into half their previous number, and new and powerful central agencies were created, with responsibility for important areas of the economy: construction, technology, and planning. Unless the political motives are taken into account, Khrushchev's policy for soviet industrial administration from 1957 to 1962 can only be described as capricious.

There is less evidence of political or economic rationality in his agricultural policy. Even in good times, Khrushchev tended to favor spectacular innovations, rather than investments in the improvement of existing facilities. When he did concern himself with the latter his indulgence for massive administrative reorganization once again revealed itself. In 1958, the network of Machine Tractor Stations was suddenly abolished. This reform was designed to eliminate costs and conflicts arising from the existence of rival bureaucracies in the countryside, although the cost of purchasing the MTS equipment which was imposed on the *kolkhozniki* could not have improved their morale and incentive. The ramifications of such drastic administrative surgery had not been fully thought out, for it was necessary only a few years later to create two new and very powerful centrally-controlled agencies—one for the purchase of machinery and the other for agricultural procurement and inspection—to supplant key functions formerly performed by the MTS.

A far more sweeping administrative reorganization of the Khrushchev era was the rapid consolidation of collective farms, the conversion of collective farms into state farms, and the build-up of new state farms in the developing eastern agricultural regions of the Soviet Union. This policy originated at the end of the Stalinist era, and had been pursued by all of Stalin's successors. The idea of gigantic agricultural communities (*agrogoroda*) or agrocities, as they were called, had been particularly dear to Khrushchev's heart for many years. Like Stalin, he also looked with favor on the *Sovkhoz* type of agricultural community, the State Farm, more directly controlled by the government. Khrushchev continued this major reform, but with much greater zeal than any leader had ever demonstrated before: he doubled the previous pace of both *kolkhoz* consolidation and the growth of state farms. This sudden acceleration of the tempo of peasant reorganization—reminiscent of Stalin's approach, although nowhere as severe—was, however, implemented with a similar lack of preparation and consequent disruption and suffering. Whole villages were obliged to pull up stakes and move themselves to other localities without adequate provision having been made for their transport. The further consolidation and regimentation of the peasant masses, if anything, had a negative effect on agricultural production. Khrushchev himself was sufficiently disillusioned with the experiment in its later years to publicly disparage the Chinese when they embarked upon their much more reckless adventure in the construction of human anthills in the countryside.

Khrushchev's solutions for the growing agricultural crisis of the last years of his rule were even more grandiose than his administrative reforms, both in the scope of their expectations and the dimensions of their failure. Perhaps the best known of these was the so-called "Virgin Lands" program. Just as the government was now promoting in earnest the industrialization of the eastern regions of the Soviet Union, Khrushchev proposed to develop their agricultural capacities. The massive cultivation of neglected but fertile lands in southern Siberia and Central Asia, presumably suitable for grain production, was to end Russia's grain shortages. Production was to double to insure a safe margin of surplus, and through the extensive colonization of the area with State Farms, a much more viable system of grain procurement would be provided. Following the Stalinist custom, a stupendous investment was poured into the new program, which was accompanied by a suitable propaganda campaign. However, as had happened so many times before, adequate technical calculations were not made. Overcultivation, without provision for adequate fallow, exhausted the soil. The climate, which was basically too dry for grain cultivation, reverted to its barren semi-arid nature after the first few years of unusually high rainfall. An initially bountiful grain crop was thus succeeded in the late 1950's and early 1960's by foreboding failures. By 1964, the Virgin Lands Program had to be acknowledged as a failure.

A similar fate was met by Khrushchev's less famous panacea for intensifying agricultural production, both in the east and in the traditional western and more northerly agricultural regions of the Soviet Union. This was the corn drive, instituted in 1955. Relatively little corn had been grown in tsarist Russia; people did not eat it, nor did they appreciate its value as animal fodder. Stalin neglected corn, as either food or silage, an oversight comparable but not exactly similar to Khrushchev's sharp curtailment of oats. Stalin, however, was disinterested in agriculture in general; Khrushchev sacrificed everything to corn. Corn was to be grown everywhere, even in those places where it could not ripen. Its main use was to serve as silage. For Khrushchev, corn became a kind of magic plant, which could not be wasted; so long as it came out of the ground, it could be used in one way or another. In fact, despite a tenfold increase in corn acreage from 1953 to 1962, much of the corn crop was badly cultivated and had to be written off as a total loss. This in turn had to be compounded with losses incurred from the cutback of other more practical crops, such as potatoes.

As a last resort, Khrushchev turned to water and fertilizers as new magical substances that would extricate Russia from her agricultural difficulties. Just before his downfall, he renewed his drive for irrigation on a large scale, and urged a new build-up of the soviet chemical industry. Like Stalin's and Khrushchev's other projects, these reforms were to be Herculean undertakings, involving tens of billions of rubles invested over periods extending several years into the future. As in so many other instances, technical details, such as the low output of artificially irrigated land, or the lag between soviet chemical technology and the ambitious program for the chemical industries that was being planned, were overlooked.

The economic rock bottom of the Khrushchev era was reached in 1962 and 1963 when the soviet government was forced into the humiliation of buying grain abroad, and of raising food prices at home. There were demonstrations, riots, and looting in several cities, in which hundreds of people were killed. These protests were put down and hushed up, but the forces had already been set in motion within the party apparatus, where Khrushchev's foreign as well as his domestic policies had consolidated factions hostile to him, to bring about his ouster. This came several months later, in the fall of 1964.

It is difficult to assess Nikita Khrushchev's place in the industrial history of Russia. His political achievements were notable; the most significant of his acts, the de-Stalinization, created the environment necessary for future economic reform. Yet Khrushchev, the de-Stalinizer, apparently could not shake off the methods and habits of economic management in which he had been trained in the Stalin era. In this respect, he must be seen as a transitional figure. It is difficult, however, from our dim knowledge of the inner workings of soviet politics, to assess the role of political pressures in prompting Khrushchev to embark on policies which frequently, from an economic point of view, seemed adventurous and impractical.

The advent of the new regime of the middle and late 1960's, marks a new course in soviet industrial history, if there are also clear signs in other aspects of government policy that have been interpreted as a return to Stalinist traditions on the part of Khrushchev's successors. For the first time in almost fifty years of communist rule in Russia—or at least since the middle 1920's—there were leaders, some of whom were experienced in economic administration and attentive to sophisticated economic thinking. One refers particularly to Aleksei Kosygin, who is generally considered to be the author of soviet economic policy and reform in the post-Khrushchevian period. Kosygin, like his predecessors of the 1950's, was a graduate of the Stalinist apparatus. He was a protégé of Stalin and Zhdanov, but more than this, Minister of the Textile Industry and a personal economic advisor of Stalin for many years. It was Kosygin who announced the reforms of 1965, which are now still in the process of implementation.

These reforms, perhaps with exaggeration, have been compared to the NEP and the *Pyatiletki* as turning points of soviet industrial history. They are nonetheless very significant, but in quite a different way than the economic programs of Lenin and Stalin. The Kosygin Reforms were not intended to make drastic alterations in the structure of society, or to retreat in the face of economic disaster, as in 1929 and 1921; and, unlike the dramatic decisions of those years, the reforms of 1965 were not made in the desperation of grave political and economic crises. They were calculated, realistic, and prudently experimental moves to rationalize the existing Soviet industrial system. The main emphasis in the Kosygin reforms was decentralization. However, this was not the pseudodecentralization of Khrushchevist, Stalinist—or tsarist—times, where new bureaucratic structures were created into which troublesome and entrenched officials could be shifted or circumvented. Rather, it was an attempt, more analogous to some of the reforms of the Leninist period, or of the tsarist Minister Stolypin (see Chapter 2), to provide more freedom, initiative, and incentive at the local level—specifically, the industrial enterprise, although also in a more limited way, the collective farm.

For the intellectual background of the Kosygin reforms, one must turn to the last part of the Khrushchev era. It was in 1962 that the most significant economic discussions in soviet Russia since the "industrialization debates" of Preobrazhensky and Bukharin were opened. The participants in these discussions were, as in the 1920's, primarily members of the economic administrative hierarchy and professional economists. The initiator of the debate, and the man whose name is popularly identified with it, was Professor Ye. G. Liberman of Kharkov University. However, the names of academicians V. Nemchinov and V. A. Trapeznikov, V. Lagutkin, Deputy Chairman of the *Sovnarkhoz* of the RSFSR, and Professors L. V. Kantorovich and V. V. Novozhilov should also be mentioned along with Liberman's.

The focus of criticism in the discussions was the problem of error and imprecision in the planning system, which had led to a host of evils and waste on a colossal scale. The destruction of much of the market economy in the 1930's created the problem of devising various calculations of price, value, and production criteria, which could substitute for the automatic and relatively precise adjustments formerly performed by the market mechanism. The calculations improvised in the Stalin era were crude and arbitrary, but viable during a period when the soviet economic structure, with all attention paid to construction, basic heavy industry, and armaments, was relatively simple. Nevertheless, even in the early stages of the industrialization drive, planning imprecision exacted a heavy toll (see Chapter 4). Nowhere was this more evident than in the primitive norm, the value of gross production, by which the performance of the individual enterprise was judged and rewarded. This led to a deterioration in the quality of goods, secret hoarding of stock, frenzied speed-ups of work to meet quotas, and various kinds of corruption to evade them. Lack of incentive to innovate or raise efficiency were other results of the quantitative production standard, as they were the consequence of rigid bureaucratic control of industry. The individual plant manager had little to say about the overall efficiency of his operation, since the allocations of raw materials, fuels, and equipment were determined largely and often inaccurately by higher and distant authorities. The values and prices of goods were also determined in an arbitrary and imprecise way; frequently meaningless prices and misleading evaluations of what was being produced by industry further confused the process of planning. As soviet industry, particularly the consumer sector, became much more complex in the 1950's, these problems became magnified.

Soviet economists and planning officials, beginning with Liberman in 1962, proposed a number of ways to eliminate these evils by making planning more precise. Basically, these boiled down to two complementary reforms. At the center, more refined methods of calculation were urged. At the plant level, it was argued that much greater efficiency would be achieved if managers had greater autonomy. It was also asserted that the use of the new economics of linear programming and input-output analysis, aided by computers, was long overdue in soviet planning. By the use of mathematical techniques, Kantorovich claimed that it would be possible to calculate a meaningful system of prices. Other writers (Lagutkin, Trapeznikov) focused on the problem of formulating a better criterion for the value of production than quantity, and proposed ways of arriving at more precise estimations of the production process and of quality.

The relaxation of bureaucratic control of industry was championed by Liberman and Nemchinov. They proposed the most "radical" reform of all the measures put forward: substitution of profit for the gross production standard at the factory level. A factory's performance would be judged by the profit it accrued, based on various calculations of its investments and sales. The workers as well as the managerial staff were to have a greater stake in the success of the enterprise through the ploughing back of profits into bonus funds and into reinvestment. At the same time, the individual plant was to have a greater voice in the formulation and implementation of its plan.

Most of these proposals were incorporated into the reform program announced by Kosygin in the fall of 1965, although the government's emphasis was much more on the provision of autonomy and incentives at the local level than on the precision of technique and calculation in the central planning agencies. It was clear that mathematics and computers would play an important role in future planning, but the dream of controlling the entire soviet economy from the center with gigantic machines had been under intensifying critical fire as another panacea. The 1965 reforms in effect acknowledged this criticism by silence in the matter of massive computerization. Its frankness in the question of managerial incentives and freedoms, particularly as regarded the resurrection of profit and interest, was not, however, an indication that the soviet reformers were moving in the direction of restoring a market economy on the basis of the NEP or capitalist systems. This interpretation, which gained currency in Western and soviet circles, was directly contradicted by the administrative aspects of the 1965 proposals, both in terms of what was changed and what was kept. The omnipresent inspectional apparatus which had been established under Stalin and Khrushchev was left very largely intact. At the same time, the ministerial system was restored to Russian industry. Thus, there was little indication in the Kosygin proposals or their subsequent implementation that state control of the Russian industrial economy was being diminished. It was the nature of this still rigorously bureaucratic system that was changing. The essence of this change, following the ideas of Liberman and Nemchinov, was to shift control of factory planning, management, and income from higher levels of the bureaucratic structure to the individual enterprise (or the numerous consolidations of enterprises, reminiscent of the trusts of the NEP period, the *firmy*, or "firms," which had been set up in recent years). This was done by basing plan performance, not on gross output, but on profits. The enterprise had a stake in its own development, not only through the use of these profits for bonuses and expansion, but also by the payment of interest on capital invested in it.

Implementation of the Kosygin reforms began almost immediately, but no attempt was made at sweeping, overnight change, so characteristic of policies of earlier eras. A preliminary reorganization was achieved in consumer industry during 1965, when 400 factories were released from their output quotas, and put into a direct relationship with retail outlets. The aim here was to improve the quality of consumer goods and the efficiency of the distribution process by creating a more immediate supply-demand relationship. In 1966, hundreds of enterprises were absorbed into the new system of managerial incentive, including machine factories, as well as manufacturers of consumer durables and food industries. In 1967, thousands more were so converted, a bloc of enterprises which produced 20 percent of total soviet industrial output. In soviet agriculture, a cautious but in many ways more positive and comprehensive program than the schemes of Khrushchev was developed. Tax relief, wage reforms, and relaxation of pressure on the private economy of the peasants was accompanied by substantial investment in agriculture. There was a trend toward greater autonomy of the collective farm analagous to the industrial reforms, although far less ambitious. By 1968, all of these reforms seem to have been firmly rooted, although military imbroglios in Eastern Europe, the Middle East, and along the Chinese-Soviet border could have the effect of reviving the wartime, mobilized, command economy and increasing the influence of its proponents.

The growth of the soviet economy in the period since 1953

has made it clear that a pattern of pronounced fluctuations was not unique to the 1930's. The leveling-off in the last few years of Stalin's rule was followed by a rather spectacular growth in the mid-1950's. By 1958, agricultural as well as industrial production had increased by about 50 percent over the level of four years before.[1] There was a much more substantial growth of consumer industry than at any time since the mid-1930's, almost 40 percent —despite costly military and space programs. The annual growth rate for industry as a whole was about 11 percent. Population and urbanization, particularly in the eastern regions, expanded rapidly. The average rate of annual increase in per capita consumption was fantastically higher than in the austere prewar years, and over twice that of several years following 1958. However, per capita income in the Soviet Union was still lower than in many Western countries.

After 1958, the annual rate of industrial growth began to slacken, more than would be considered normal at that stage of development. It dropped from 10.6 percent (1950–1958 average) to 7.3 percent in the last three years of Khrushchev's rule. By the beginning of 1970, although heavy industry continued to grow at previous rates, there was less impressive growth, compared to the mid-1950's, in many consumer industries, and a mounting crisis in soviet agriculture. Khrushchev's erratic policies, which drained so much investment into unproductive projects, must be seen as one of the causes for this slump. However, underlying his blunders and, most recently, the failure of the reforms initiated by his successors to live up to expectations, must be seen three longer-range factors: persisting defects in the planning system, the backwardness of soviet agriculture, and an expensive military-space program. It is a sign of the realism of the current leadership that it has resolutely attacked the first two of these problems. The third, as everywhere, is less sus-

[1] Figures for this period are derived from Harry Schwartz, *The Soviet Economy Since Stalin;* Herbert Levine, "Industry" in *Prospects for Soviet Society;* and James Blackman, "The Kosygin Reforms: New Wine in Old Bottles," in *The Development of the Soviet Economy: Plan and Performance.* See bibliography for Chapter 5.

ceptible to rational control, and may in the long run prove to be—as so often before in Russian history—a major brake on Russian progress.

CONCLUSION: RUSSIAN TRADITION AND SOVIET INDUSTRIALIZATION

Soviet industrialization must be recognized as one of outstanding economic accomplishments as well as one of the most important events of modern times. In what perspective may it best be understood? It has been most frequently viewed within the context of Western European and American experience. This is instructive and necessary, although misleading, particularly when comparative analysis becomes a disguise for judgments about the inferiority or superiority of one system or people to another. Unfortunately, such judgments have formed one of the main themes of Russian and Western thought since at least the time of the nineteenth-century Slavophiles. Even in very recent times, much commentary on soviet economic development has not been immune to such biases. In any event, since comparison with the West remains the dominant concern of interpreters of soviet industrialization, it must be given critical consideration.

The first comparison that is always made for soviet industrialization is with capitalism. The differences between the two methods of industrialization are frequently emphasized and much evidence and argument have been accumulated to demonstrate both the merits and the weaknesses of planning and other soviet innovations as compared to capitalist institutions. However, the similarities of the two industrial revolutions are also significant. In both cases, there was a rapid and massive transformation of society from agriculture to industry. In the case of some capitalist countries, such as England, the comparison with soviet industrialization extends to the fact that economic development came about relatively free of foreign influence or control. That the Soviet Union was able to achieve rapid industrial growth, the military power, and material wealth of the capitalist societies, yet with a backward peasant society, lack of a strong middle class, and other traditions and attitudes integral to capitalist development, and to do this avoiding imperialist exploitation, would indicate it as a model for many underdeveloped countries in Africa and Asia with similar institutions and problems. Yet, unlike many advanced capitalist societies, per capita income at this advanced stage of Soviet industrialization remains very low.

This points up the fact that in terms of exploitation and suffering on a mass scale, the soviet and capitalist methods of industrialization have been very similar. Whether this misery was necessary or inevitable is one of the most difficult of historical questions to answer with any finality. Answers change with the times. Certainly, both systems have inspired their "dismal economists" to argue that most of the respective evils could not have been avoided, given certain circumstances and goals. And both systems have produced critics, who have argued the opposite; while many critics of one system, of course, have sympathized with the other. And, just as the evils of early capitalism, when somewhat modified, changed the thinking of its socialist critics, so the evils and virtues of soviet industrialization have changed the thinking of its procapitalist critics. Indeed, views of capitalism have changed with changes in soviet industrial history.[2] This was not simply a matter of the political prejudices of the historians of capitalism, but of fact. As suffering intensified in soviet Russia, capitalism naturally looked better; and, as soviet economic power burgeoned, capitalism looked worse.

Comparisons are also frequently made between soviet industrialization and socialism, a much more complex and confusing issue. It is partially a semantic one, since one must always ask: What variety or perversion of socialism? To view soviet industrialization as a mere masquerade of socialism, as has often been done, would be naive, although a case can be built against the claim that soviet industrialization was socialistic. Lenin was quite frank about this in his characterization of War

[2] See the article by E. H. Carr, "Some Random Reflections on Soviet Industrialization," in *Socialism, Capitalism and Economic Growth* (Cambridge, 1967), 271–84.

Communism and the NEP. And in Marxian terms themselves, it could be argued (and was, in Russia, until the theories were suppressed by Stalin) that the Georgian dictator was not creating socialism, but restoring the primitive Marxian "Oriental Mode of Production" or, as Bukharin more aptly described it at the time, "military feudalism." But the fact is that socialist thinking has played and continues to play an important role in soviet industrialization. Many soviet leaders conceived of themselves as socialists, if they acted otherwise; and although socialist ideology has frequently been ignored or perverted, no serious attempt has been made to jettison it. Finally socialist ideas have helped to shape soviet economic institutions, although they may not have been the primary determinants of what was created. The question is whether the most effective way of understanding soviet industrialization is through the study of socialist teachings. It is the opinion of this author that to view soviet industrialization either as an institutionalization of socialist ideas, or to measure it by the standard of Western capitalism are not the most productive lines of inquiry.

One of the purposes of this essay has been to try to indicate a third line of inquiry, that of historical perspective. From this point of view, it is more enlightening to view soviet industralization within the context of Russian tradition. Rather than compare soviet industrialization with capitalism or socialism, when we place it in the historical perspective of the tsarist economy and society, a clearer pattern emerges, and one which is freer, it may be suggested, of semantical confusions and myths.

What was the Russian tradition, which manifested itself in both tsarist and soviet economic development? It would be meaningless to define this tradition, as has often been done, in such simplistic terms as the persistence of "habit" or national "traits"; and it would make even less sense to attach great importance to carry-overs from the governing structure and personnel of the old regime into the new order, or to soviet copies of tsarist procedures and symbols, although there is evidence of this superficial kind of continuity. Tradition consists of institutions and modes of behavior produced over long periods of time by relatively static conditions; they die hard, and if the conditions persist, then there will be even greater continuity. There were geographic, economic, and strategic conditions which persisted through the tsarist and soviet periods, which, as they were modified and intensified during alternating periods of stability and stress in the twentieth century, perpetuated traditions.[3]

At least five such traditions functioned during the industrialization of Russia in the tsarist and soviet periods. They may be identified as: Bureaucracy, Military Mobilization, The Tribute System, Slavery, and Violence.

Bureaucracy: This is one of the most deep-rooted of Russian traditions, a result of strategic and economic conditions that were present at the time of the formation of the Russian state. Excessive defense requirements occasioned by Russia's exposure to numerous, militarily superior enemies, and imposed on a vast, geographically uniform, and underpopulated northern plain, a land normally too poor to bear such a burden, necessitated the creation of a massive centralized bureaucratic apparatus, controlling strong military and police components with which to organize the nation for survival. This machine grew over the centuries, and developed a kind of independent and self-regenerative power. It was not smashed to pieces by the revolution, but in fact merged with the Communist Party bureaucracy. The persistence and intensification of the conditions of poverty and war which had created it, combined with the anarchical conditions issuing from the revolution, resulted in the growth of even greater, more arbitrary, and highly centralized bureaucratic power. Bureaucratic control extended to embrace every facet of soviet economic life. The Plan, with its centralized command system, its huge administrative apparatus, and complex network of inspectional agencies, was a natural expression of this tradition.

Military Mobilization: Military threats to Russia were of such severity throughout her history, frequently resulting in actual invasion of the country and wholesale devastation, that they oc-

[3] A fuller analysis of Russian tradition and the conditions which determined it is found in the first part of Chapter 1.

casioned not only the maintenance of a large military establishment with all the trappings of militarism, but also massive mobilization efforts. The idea of total mobilization for war, even for extended periods in peacetime, became an accepted fact of life, and a policy facilitated by the concentration of autocratic power in the hands of a semimilitarized tsar or dictator. In the psychology of the more dynamic of the autocrats, total mobilization was expressed by an extreme voluntarism bordering on megalomania, a heightened belief in the power of the human will to effect profound change in history, and as a corollary to this, the willingness to inflict and to demand tremendous sacrifices of the people. Three such mobilizations took place in the soviet period, two in time of war (1917–1921, 1940–1945), and one in time of peace (1929–1935). In modern times, such mobilizations meant forced industrialization, as in the cases of the Petrine reforms, the industrialization drive following the Crimean War, and the Stalinist industrialization. Involvement in war has frequently strained the economy to the breaking point; and the cost of maintaining a huge war machine has always worked to seriously weaken the industrialization effort. These tensions have led to periodic crises or even revolutions.

The Tribute System: The two primary sources of Russia's wealth have been grain and peasant labor. Other sources of revenue were secondary or insignificant during most of her history. To finance the war machine and the various industrialization efforts, it was necessary to extract a very large tribute from the peasantry, far beyond what they were ordinarily willing and able to pay. Force was used to oblige them to produce the requisite surpluses. Several systems of tribute were employed in modern times, ranging from the *obrok* and *barschina,* which developed in the late Muscovite period, to the more recent obligatory grain deliveries of the Stalinist collective farms. With the growth of markets in the past two centuries, heavy indirect taxation of the consumer has gained increasing importance as a means of state revenue. A third of the revenue of the tsarist government during the nineteenth century was derived from the drinking tax; and a much higher proportion of soviet revenue during the Stalinist industrialization drive came from the turn-over tax.

Slavery: A chronic shortage of labor was characteristic of tsarist and soviet times. The causes were similar: underpopulation, bad times economically, political instability, war, the chronic migration of peasants and urban workers, and the underutilization and unsuitability of rural labor. This labor shortage was met by various systems of permanent or temporary forced labor, ranging from outright slavery and hereditary serfdom, to various forms of conscription, corvées, internal passport systems, and rigid factory discipline. The system of group rather than individual responsibility (*krugovaya poruka*), which the tsars had employed for centuries as a way of insuring fulfillment through mutual coercion of work quotas and other obligations imposed by the state, was restored under Stalin in name as well as in substance in various forms for factories, farms, and labor camps. Forced labor of political prisoners was also characteristic of both the tsarist and soviet systems. However, it was employed on a much vaster scale by the latter regime during its industrialization drive, partly as a legacy of massive political terror, but also because it assumed an important economic function, not only in construction projects that might otherwise not have been undertaken, but in helping to depress consumption by the elimination of millions of buyers from the market.

Violence: Violence, both institutionalized (wars, police purges) and spontaneous (revolutionary conspiracies, riots, terrorism, brigandage) has long been a part of the Russian tradition, as of the traditions of most other countries. However, in the past century, violence in all the above forms became particularly acute in Russia. Men habituated to cruelty and criminal acts were able to enter and even to dominate public life in such an environment; this in turn resulted in the brutalization of policy and decision-making, particularly those decisions which concerned industrial mobilization. These far over-stepped those bounds of humanity and legality which had restrained governments in normal times, and which had been respected by the majority of the revolutionary forces as well.

In the context of Russian tradition so understood, the appearance of Stalin is explainable. Stalin was not inevitable, neither was he accidental. Stalin remade Russia into the second military and economic power of the world, but at a tremendous cost in human suffering. The extent to which his achievements compensate for the costs is the main determinant of how necessary Stalin was. Stalin did not create a socialist welfare society, but he did create a viable economic system, whose permanence is assured by its accord with Russian traditions of state power. How widely applicable Stalin's system will be, as a method of disproportionate, crash modernization, for other peasant societies of similar inertias, but with traditions less brutal and despotic than those of Russia, is a question still being debated by economists. In the essentials perhaps, "Russia never changes"; but the harshness and rigidity of the iron age of Stalinist industrialization are already beginning to pass. It is reasonable to expect that two generations hence, soviet Russia will be as far from Stalinism as the Russia of Tolstoi's *War and Peace* was different from the crude times of Peter the Great. It is much less probable, although not impossible, that over the course of another century, a westernized, liberalized society comparable to the "capitalist" Russia of the pre-World War 1 period would be reconstructed. Despite clear, if timid, signs of a debureaucratization of the soviet economy, it is also possible that growing military involvements and the threat of war could bring on a new economic mobilization and with it, a new Stalinism.

Glossary of
Russian Terms
and Designations

Agrogorod. Agricultural city, a type of huge state farm promoted in the 1950's.

Apparatchik. A soviet organization man.

Bednyak. A poor peasant.

Birzha. A commercial exchange or stock market of tsarist times.

Blat. "Pull," covert influence to obtain contracts, supplies, and other necessities in the soviet industrial system.

Chastnik. A soviet private entrepreneur of the NEP period, a "Nepman."

Chervonetz. Monetary unit established in 1922.

Firm. A consolidation of industrial enterprises.

Glavk, Glavki. Abbreviation for Main Administrations, agencies controlling early soviet industries.

GOELRO. State Commission for the Electrification of Russia, an early soviet planning agency.

Gosplan. State Planning Commission, founded in 1921.

Gostinnii Dvor. A permanent urban market place in tsarist Russia.

GULAG. Main Administration of Camps, an agency of the NKVD, in charge of the forced labor camps.

Khozrashchot. Business accounting, a form of accountability and autonomy for the individual enterprise for purchases and sales, established in 1921.

Kolkhoz. A collective farm.

173

Kombedy.   Committees of the Poor, functioned in the Civil War to confiscate grain.

Kontraktsiya.   Contract, a system of compulsory prearranged grain sales at prices lower than the market, used during the early years of the collectivization drive.

Krugovaya Poruka.   Group responsibility, a system in which the group bears responsibility for fulfillment of individual tax and labor obligations.

Kulak.   A well-to-do peasant.

NEP.   The New Economic Policy, introduced in 1921.

NKVD.   People's Commissariat of Internal Affairs, name of the secret police in the 1930's. See OGPU, GULAG.

OGPU.   Unified State Political Administration, name of the secret police during the early years of the Stalinist industrialization drive.

Perekachka.   "Pumping," extracting surpluses from the peasants through fixed quotas, low prices, taxes, and other forms of requisition.

Prodnalog.   Produce tax, a levy on agricultural produce, substituted for confiscation in 1921.

Prodotryad.   Produce Detachment, armed units which functioned in the Civil War to confiscate grain.

Prodrazverstka.   Produce Requisition, the grain confiscation policy of the Civil War period.

Pyatilyetka.   A five-year plan.

Sbor s Oborota.   The turnover tax, a high indirect tax levied on most goods sold in the Soviet Union, established in 1930.

Serednyak.   A peasant of moderate means.

Sovkhoz.   A state farm.

Sovnarkhoz.   Regional Council of the National Economy, an administrative agency set up in the 1950's.

Sovznak.   Soviet token, collective designation for the several types of soviet rubles issued during the Civil War and the early NEP period.

Sploshnaya Kollektivizatsiya.   Crash, or rapid, and forced collectivization of the peasants, undertaken late in 1929.

Tolkach. "Pusher," an expediter of supplies through the soviet industrial bureaucracy.

Trudoden. Workday, a system of compensation for labor performed by peasants for their collective farms.

Tryest. Trust, a grouping of factories employed in the NEP period and in more recent times.

Tsekh. Shop or guild, a craft organization in tsarist times, a shop within a factory in the soviet period.

Udarnik. A shock worker.

Vesenkha. Supreme Council of the National Economy, established December, 1917.

Yarmarka. A fair.

Bibliographical Essay

This is a selected bibliography of the most important books and articles on the subject of Russian industrialization written in the English and Russian languages (with a few very important items in French and German). The scholarship and documentation untranslated from Russian is enormous. What has been included here is of necessity highly selective. Fuller bibliographies can be found in almost any of the works cited. A few interesting or important published primary sources for each period have been included.

CHAPTER 1 / PREINDUSTRIAL RUSSIA

Although political histories of Russia abound, there are few general economic histories of that country which are comprehensive and up-to-date. A similar lacuna exists for the history of Russian agriculture and industry. The most famous, and the best, survey of the economic development of the Russian empire to the revolution of 1917 is Peter I. Lyashchenko, *History of the National Economy of Russia to 1917* (New York, 1949). The Russian original of this work, written from a soviet Marxist point of view, has a third volume dealing with the Communist period. See Peter I. Lyashchenko, *Istoriya narodnovo khozyaistva S S S R,* 4th ed. (Moscow, 1956), 3 vols. An excellent and comprehensive summary of the first thousand years of Russian agrarian history can be found in Jerome Blum, *Lord and Peasant in Russia from the Ninth to the Nineteenth Century* (Princeton, 1961). In the past few generations no general history of Russian industry has been written that supersedes Mikhail I. Tugan-Baranovsky's, *Russkaya fabrika v proshlom i nastoyashchem* (*The Russian Factory in the Past and Present*), (St. Petersburg, 1898), Vol. I. There is a German translation of this classic: *Geschichte der Russischen-fabrik* (Berlin, 1900).

The most brilliant exposition of the traditional Russian despotism, and of its economic foundations and characteristics, remains Georgii V. Plekhanov's introductory essay to his *Istoriya Russkoi obshchestvennoi mysli* (*History of Russian Social Thought*), (Moscow, 1914), Vol. I, with a French translation: *Introduction à l'histoire sociale de la Russie* (Paris, 1926). An important reassessment of the basis of Russian economic backwardness is Alexander Baykov, "The Economic Development of Russia," *Economic History Review*, 2nd series, VII (1954), 137–49; see also the first chapter of Holland Hunter, *Soviet Transportation Policy* (Harvard, 1957). A short and suggestive soviet summary can be found in A. Abramov, *Prichiny ekonomicheskoi otstal'nosti tsarskoi Rossii* (*Causes of the Economic Backwardness of Tsarist Russia*), (Leningrad, 1941). The best known general approach to the periodization of economic growth, which draws upon the Russian experience in discussing the traditional society and the period of preparation for rapid industrial development, is Walt W. Rostow, *The Stages of Economic Growth* (Cambridge, 1960). For a much broader conceptualization of the transition to modernity, which also draws upon the Russian example and shows a keener appreciation of the influence of political tradition, see C. E. Black, *The Dynamics of Modernization* (New York, 1966).

The most authoritative soviet studies of the preindustrial accumulation of capital in Russia are Lyubomir G. Beskrovny, ed., *K voprosu pervonachalnom nakoplenii v Rossii* (*xvii–xviii vv.*), (*The Problem of the Original Accumulation of Capital in Russia, 17th–18th centuries*), (Moscow, 1958); and Fedor Ya. Polyansky, *Pervonachal'noe nakoplenie kapitala v Rossii* (*The Original Accumulation of Capital in Russia*), (Moscow, 1958). A short summary and criticism of these ideas is presented in the article by Alexander Gershenkron, "Rosario Romeo and the Original Accumulation of Capital," *Economic Backwardness in His-*

torical Perspective (New York, 1965), 90–118. Russian industrial development in the seventeenth and eighteenth centuries can best be viewed in the following studies: Andrei A. Vvedensky, *Dom Stroganovykh v XVI–XVII Vekakh* (*The House of Stroganov in the XVI–XVII Centuries*), (Moscow, 1962); Yelena I. Zaozerskaya, *Manufaktura pri Petra I* (*Manufacturing Enterprises Under Peter I*), (Moscow-Leningrad, 1947); Arcadius Kahan, "Continuity in Economic Activity and Policy During the Post-Petrine Period in Russia," *Journal of Economic History,* XXV (1965), 61–85; and by the same author, "The Costs of 'Westernization' in Russia: The Gentry and the Economy in the Eighteenth Century," *Slavic Review,* XXV (1966), 40–46; Berngard B. Kafengauz, *Istoriya khozyaistva Demidovykh XVIII–XIX vv.* (*History of the Demidov Economy, 18th–19th Centuries*), (Moscow-Leningrad, 1949), Vol. I; and Roger Portal, *L'Oural au XVIIIe siecle* (Paris, 1950).

The subject of industrial development in Russia during the early nineteenth century is surveyed in William L. Blackwell, *The Beginnings of Russian Industrialization 1800–1860* (Princeton, 1968); and Mariya K. Rozhkova, ed., *Ocherki ekonomicheskoi istorii Rossii pervoi poloviny XIX veka* (*Essays on the Economic History of Russia in the First Half of the Nineteenth Century*), (Moscow, 1959). It is also discussed on the symposia, *Genezis kapitalizma v promyshlennosti* (*The Genesis of Capitalism in Industry*), (Moscow, 1963); and *Voprosy genezisa kapitalizma v Rossii*), (*Problems of the Genesis of Capitalism in Russia*), (Leningrad, 1960). State policy as it affected industry in the second quarter of the nineteenth century is considered in Walter Pintner, *Russian Economic Policy Under Nicholas I* (Cornell, 1967); and the history of Russian science and technology in the eighteenth and early nineteenth centuries, in Alexander Vucinich, *Science in Russian Culture* (Stanford, 1963).

A fairly comprehensive bibliography of the numerous published primary sources for the history of Russian industry in the eighteenth and nineteenth centuries can be found in the study by Blackwell, cited above, 437–443. The following few materials might be singled out as having particular importance: *Arkhiv grafov Mordvinovykh* (*Archive of the Counts Mordvinov*), (St. Petersburg, 1901–1903), 10 vols.; *Dnevnye dozornye zapisi o Moskovskikh raskol'nikakh, Chteniya v imperatorskom obshchestve istorii i drevnostei Rossiiskikh* (*Daily Patrol Reports on the Moscow Schismatics, Proceedings of the Imperial Society of Russian History and Antiquities*), to be found in the supplements for 1885, 1886, and 1892; and Dmitry Milyutin, "Ob opastnosti prodolzheniya v 1856 voennykh deistvii," ("On the Dangers of Continuing Military Activities in 1856"), a memorandum printed in *Istoricheskii arkhiv* (*Historical Archive*), (1959), 206–8. There are practically no primary sources on Russian industrialization before 1860 published in languages other than Russian. Mention should be made, however, of Baron A. von Haxthausen's important contemporary analysis, *The Russian Empire, Its People, Institutions and Resources* (English edition, London, 1856), 2 vols., which has recently been reprinted.

CHAPTER 2 / THE FIRST INDUSTRIALIZATION DRIVE, 1856–1913

There are some good surveys of the industrial development of Russia during the reigns of the last three tsars in the books by Pavel A. Khromov, *Ekonomicheskoe Razvitie Rossii v XIX–XX vekakh* (*The Economic Development of Russia in the 19th and 20th Centuries*), (Moscow, 1950); *Ekonomika Rossii, period promyshlennovo kapitalizma* (*The Economy of Russia, Period of Industrial Capitalism*), (Moscow, 1963); and *Ocherki Ekonomiki Rossii Perioda Monopoliticheskovo Kapitalizma* (*Essays on the Economic History of Russia in the Period of Monopolistic Capitalism*), (Moscow, 1960). There is also a comprehensive and brief analysis in the article by Roger Portal "The Industrialization of Russia," in the *Cambridge Economic History of Europe* (Cambridge, 1965), Vol. VI, 801–74. For economists' assessments of tsarist industrial growth, see Raymond Goldsmith, "The Economic Growth of Tsarist Russia 1860–1913," *Economic Development and Cultural Change*, IX (1961), 441–75; and Alexander Gershenkron, "The Rate of Industrial Growth in Russia Since 1885,"

Tasks of Economic History, Journal of Economic History (1947), Supplement VII.

An excellent account of the impact of agrarian policy on impeding and facilitating economic growth can be found in the same volume of the Cambridge History cited above, in the article by Alexander Gershenkron, "Agrarian Policies and Industrialization: Russia, 1861–1917," 706–800. The Stolypin reforms are outlined in greater detail in G. T. Robinson, *Rural Russia Under the Old Regime* (New York, 1932); and G. L. Yaney, "The Concept of the Stolypin Land Reform," *Slavic Review*, XXIII (1964), 275–93. On state industrial and fiscal policy, see Theodore H. Von Laue, *Sergei Witte and the Industrialization of Russia* (New York, 1963); and Olga Crisp, "Russian Financial Policy and the Gold Standard at the End of the Nineteenth Century," *Economic History Review*, 2nd series, VI (1953).

For a brief summary of the history of state and private banking in the late tsarist period, see the article by the same author in Rondon Cameron, ed., *Banking in the Early Stages of Industrialization* (New York, 1967); and an authoritative soviet study, I. F. Gindin, *Russkie Kommercheskie Banki* (*Russian Commercial Banks*), (Moscow, 1948). For insurance, consult Paul Best, "The Origins and Development of Insurance in Imperial and Soviet Russia" (Unpublished doctoral dissertation, New York University, 1965). On railroads, there is the recent survey by John N. Westwood, *A History of Russian Railways* (London, 1964). Russian capitalism is beginning to receive attention from scholars within and outside of the Soviet Union. The older soviet study was Pavel A. Berlin, *Russkaya burzhuaziya v staroe i nove vremya* (*The Russian Bourgeoisie in Past and Recent Times* (Moscow, 1922). A general survey was written in the United States by Valentine Bill, *The Forgotten Class* (New York, 1959). More recently I. F. Gindin has published the series of articles entitled, "Russkaya Burzhuaziya v Period Kapitalizma Yeyo Razvitie i Osobennosti ("The Russian Bourgeoisie in the Period of Capitalism, Its Development and Peculiarities"), *Istoriya S S S R* (*History of the U.S.S.R.*) (1963), Nos. 2 and 3, among numerous other articles and monographs. The old Russian industrialists publicized themselves widely and, among many works, one should note C. Yoksimovich, *Manufakturnaya promyshlennost v proshlom i nastoyashchem* (*The Manufacturing Industry in Past and Present*), (Moscow, 1915), Vol. I. The emergence of the Jewish industrial entrepreneur is discussed briefly by Salo Baron, *The Russian Jew Under Tsars and Soviets* (New York, 1964); the Moscovite textile industrialists by Roger Portal, "Industriels Moscovites: le Secteur Cotonnier (1861–1914)," *Cahiers du Monde Russe et Sovietique*, IV (1963), 5–46; and the foreign entrepreneur by Eric Amburger, "Der fremde Unternehmer in Russland bis zur Oktoberrevolution im Jahre 1917," *Tradition, Zeitschrift für Firmengeschichte und Unternehmerbiographie*, 2nd year (1957), No. 4, 337–55. Foreign enterprise and investment in Russia during the last decades of the tsarist period can be studied in Boris F. Brandt, *Industrannyye Kapitaly* (*Foreign Capital*), (St. Petersburg, 1898–99), Part 2; and Anton Crihan, *Le Capital Etranger en Russie* (Paris, 1934). For Russian technology during the same period, see Viktor V. Danilevsky, *Russkaya Tekhnika* (Moscow, 1948); and A. A. Zvorikine, "Remarques sur l'histoire des inventions et de la pensée scientifique et technique russes des XVIIIᵉ et XIXᵉ siecles," *Contributions a l'histoire russe, cahiers d'histoire mondiale*, special issue (1958), 183–211. On economic thought of the period as it pertained to the industrialization question, see Arthur Mendel, *Dilemmas of Progress in Tsarist Russia* (Harvard, 1961).

Of primary sources which provide interesting first hand evidence of the state economy and private capitalism in the last years of the old regime, one should consult the following memoirs: Sergei Yu. Witte, *Memoirs of Count Witte* (London, 1921); Vladimir N. Kokovtsov, *Out of My Past* (Stanford, 1935); and P. A. Buryshkin, *Moskva kupecheskaya* (*Mercantile Moscow*), (New York, 1954).

CHAPTER 3 / INDUSTRIAL DISINTEGRATION, 1914–1929

The number of monographs in English dealing with the industrial history of Russia during the First World War, revolution, civil war, and the period of the NEP is substantially greater than the number available dealing with the previous two hundred years of Russian industrial development. First, and most notably, we have the several volumes of the *Social and Economic History of the World War*, Russian Series (Carnegie Endowment for International Peace), of which the following are essential for an understanding of the industrial history of Russia during the war: Stanislav Kohn and Alexander F. Meyendorf, *The Cost of the War to Russia* (New Haven, 1932); Semen O. Zagorsky, *State Control of Industry in Russia During the War* (New Haven, 1928); Alexander M. Mikhelson, *Russian Public Finance During the War* (New Haven, 1928); and M. T. Florinsky, *The End of the Russian Empire* (New Haven, 1931), a summary volume for the series. Russian studies of the effect of the war on the economy are Sergei N. Prokopovich, *Voina i Narodnoe khozyaistvo* (*The War and the National Economy*), (Moscow, 1918), and Ivan V. Maevsky, *Ekonomika Russkoi Promyshlennosti v Usloviyakh Pervoi mirovoi voiny* (*The Economic Condition of Russian Industry in the First World War*), (Moscow, 1957). For Russian purchases of armaments in America see Lebedev, *Russo-Amerikanskie ekonomicheskie otnoshenie 1900–1917 gg.* (*Russian-American Economic Relations, 1900–1917*), (Moscow, 1964). Primary sources for the Russian wartime economy are too numerous to summarize. There are several collections in the *Krasnyi arkhiv* (*Red Archive*), and for the period of the Provisional Government, Robert P. Browder and Alexander F. Kerensky, eds., *Documents of the Provisional Government* (Stanford, 1961), 3 vols. The only study specifically of the economic policies of the Provisional Government is a soviet one, P. V. Volodyev, *Ekonomicheskaya politika vremmenoye pravitelstvo* (*The Economic Policy of the Provisional Government*), (Moscow, 1962).

On the early period of Bolshevik rule—the period of the Civil War, or "War Communism," and the early part of the New Economic Policy (NEP)—we first encounter the wide divergence of opinion that characterizes all writing about the soviet economy. On the one hand, in Lev. N. Kritsman, *Geroicheskii period velikoi russkoi revolyutsii* (*The Heroic Period of the Great Russian*

Revolution), (Moscow, 1925), we find incredible idealization of the policies of War Communism. Sergei N. Prokopovich, writing about the first six years of the soviet economy, *The Economic Condition of Soviet Russia* (London, 1924), sees Bolshevik policy in the Civil War and NEP periods, not as the foundation of socialism, but as a descent into chaos, and urges the restoration of capitalism as the only viable solution to Russia's problems. More balanced is the monumental work by an historian, E. H. Carr, who devotes about a third of his six-volume history to economic questions in the Civil War and early NEP period. See his *Bolshevik Revolution* (London, 1952), Vol. II., *Interregnum* (London, 1960), and *Socialism in One Country* (London, 1958), Vol. I. For the recent official soviet view of the NEP period, which sees a steady progress to socialism under the leadership of Lenin despite the opposition of left and right wing deviations, see Ivan A. Gladkov, *Ocherki sovetskoi Ekonomikii 1917–1920 gg.* (*Essays on the Soviet Economy 1917–1920*), (Moscow, 1956); *Sovietskoe narodnoe khozyaistvo v 1921–1925 gg.* (*The Soviet People's Economy 1921–1925*), (Moscow, 1960). The best account of the late NEP period, see Ivan V. Maevsky, *Tyazholaya promyshlennost S S S R Russian Peasants and Soviet Power* (London, 1968), by M. Lewin. On heavy industrial development in the last part of the NEP period, see Ivan V. Maevsky, *Tyazholaya promyshlennost S S S R v pervyye gody sotsialisticheskoi industrializatsii* (*1926–1929*), (*Heavy Industry of the U.S.S.R. in the First Years of Socialist Industrialization 1926–1929*), (Moscow, 1959). The more specialized topics of financial policy and currency are surveyed in English translation in Grigory Ya. Sokolnikov, *Soviet Policy in Public Finance 1917–1928* (Stanford, 1931); and L. N. Yurovsky, *Currency Problems and Policy of the Soviet Union* (London, 1925); see also Arthur Z. Arnold, *Banks, Credit and Money in Soviet Russia* (Columbia, 1937).

Soviet scholars have published recently a substantial documentation for the economic history of the Civil War and NEP periods, most notably, the collections of sources edited by Ivan A. Gladkov, *Natsionalizatsiya promyshlennosti v S S S R, 1917–1920 gg.* (*The Nationalization of Industry in the U.S.S.R. 1917–*

1920), (Moscow, 1954); *K istorii plana elektrifikatsii sovietskoi strany, 1918–1922 gg.* (*Toward a History of the Electrification Plan for the Soviet Land 1918–1922*), (GIPL, 1952); and *Razvitiye elektrifikatsii sovietskoi strany 1921–1925 gg.* (*The Development of Electrification in the Soviet Land 1921–1925*), (Moscow, 1956). See also, M. P. Kim, editor, *Pervyye shagi industrializatsii S S S R 1926–1927* (*The First Steps of the Industrialization of the U.S.S.R. 1926–1927*), (Moscow, 1959). Finally, one should consult Lenin's *Sochineniya* (*Works*), 4th edition, particularly volumes 32 and 33 (GIPL, 1950), which cover the crucial period of the late Civil War and early NEP.

CHAPTER 4 / THE SECOND INDUSTRIALIZATION DRIVE, 1929–1953

The extreme diversity of opinion about the Stalinist industrialization drive is revealed in almost every type of literature and analysis dealing with the subject. Of works treating the subject as a whole radically different pictures emerge. Nowhere can the contrast be seen better than in the two most notable general studies by economists, Maurice Dobb's *Soviet Economic Development Since 1917* (London, 1966), and Naum Jasny's *Soviet Industrialization 1928–1952* (Chicago, 1961). Dobb's work was a pioneer one in the field (first edition, 1928), an internationally received survey written from a Marxist point of view, sympathetic to soviet endeavors. Jasny's work is the more solid of the two, in the opinion of this author, both in terms of its extensive and critical use of Russian sources, and the strength of its conclusions. A more successful attempt at balance is the economist Alec Nove's very recent and detailed *An Economic History of the U.S.S.R.* (London, 1969), which devotes itself largely to the Stalin period.

An even more marked disparity of opinion can be observed among the more personal accounts of soviet Russia during the industrialization drive. To the fantasy of Sidney and Beatrice Webb, *Soviet Communism: A New Civilization?* (1935), must be contrasted the nightmare of Victor Kravchenko, *I Chose Free-*

dom (New York, 1946). Three other accounts based on individual experience that should be noted are the memoirs of an American engineer who worked at Magnitogorsk, John Scott, *Beyond the Urals* (New York, 1942); the analysis by an American journalist, long resident in Stalin's Russia, William H. Chamberlin, *Russia's Iron Age* (London, 1935); and the novel by Alexander Solzhenitsyn, *The First Circle* (New York, 1968). A famous, and far more optimistic, fictional view of the industrialization drive can be read in Valentin Katayev's *Time Forward* (New York, 1933). Of soviet histories of the industrialization drive, there is the third volume of the older work by P. I. Lyashchenko, cited in the bibliography to Chapter 1; and the more recent studies, with some revisions of Stalinist literature, by Ivan A. Gladkov, *Postroieniya fundamenta ekonomiki v S S S R 1926–1932* (*Construction of the Fundamentals of the Economy in the U.S.S.R. 1926–1932*), (Moscow, 1960) and *Sotsialisticheskoe Narodnoe Khozyaistvo S S S R 1933–1940 gg.* (*The Socialist Peoples Economy of the U.S.S.R. 1933–1940*), (Moscow, 1963). Out of the massive literature on Stalin and his apparatus, two works should be mentioned as bearing special relevance for this study: Isaac Deutscher, *Stalin: A Political Biography* (New York, 1949), which gives the best analysis of Stalin's accumulation of power; and Milovan Djilas, *Conversations with Stalin* (New York, 1962), the most penetrating insight we have into the man and his character.

Alexander Erlich, *The Soviet Industrialization Debates 1924–1928* (Harvard, 1960) is a comprehensive study of the economic issues and solutions propounded by soviet leaders and economists in the NEP period. Preobrazhensky's ideas appear translated in *The New Economics* (London, 1965); and some of Bukharin's earlier speculations in *The ABC of Communism* (Ann Arbor, 1966). A short review and critique of the official and other interpretations of the decision to collectivize is provided by Herbert G. Ellison, "The Decision to Collectivize Agriculture," *American Slavic and East European Review*, XX (1961), 189–202. A recent, exhaustive study of the economic and motivational background of the collectivization policy is the book mentioned previously by M. Lewin, *Russian Peasants and Soviet Power*. The debate which took place among English economists in the early 1960's over the necessity of Stalin's agrarian and industrialization policies is reprinted in Alec Nove, *Economic Rationality and Soviet Politics, or Was Stalin Really Necessary?* (New York, 1964), 17–39. The classic study of the collectivization itself is Naum Jasny, *The Socialized Agriculture of the U.S.S.R.* (Stanford, 1949). Official documents on the period can be found in *Kollekivizatsiya sel'skovo khozyaistva* (*The Collectivization of the Agricultural Economy*), (Moscow, 1957); and an account of personal experiences in F. Belov, *The History of a Collective Farm* (New York, 1955). The turnover tax and other forms of soviet taxation are examined in F. Holzman, *Soviet Taxation* (Harvard, 1955); Robert W. Davies' *The Soviet Budgetary System* (Cambridge, 1958) is a good coverage of budgetary matters in general, as these matters were related to the industrialization program. Housing during the plan era is described in the monograph by Timothy Sosnovy, *The Housing Problem in the Soviet Union* (New York, 1954); labor—wages, hours, conditions— in Solomon Schwarz, *Labor in the Soviet Union* (London, 1953); the role of the trade unions in the industrialization drive, Isaac Deutscher, *Soviet Trade Unions* (New York, 1950); an estimate of real wages during the Stalin period, Janet Chapman, *Real Wages in the Soviet Union* (Harvard, 1963). Out of the extensive literature on forced labor in the 1930's and 1940's, three studies should be noted: the pioneer work of David Dallin and Boris Nikolaevsky, *Forced Labor in Soviet Russia* (London, 1948); the detailed study by Paul Barton, *L'Institution concentrationnaire en Russie 1930–1957* (1959); and the very comprehensive and lucid economic analysis of the role of forced labor in the Stalinist type of industrialization, by Stanislaw Swianiewicz, an economist and a former prisoner, *Forced Labour and Economic Development* (London, 1965). On the mobilization of literature and the arts for industrialization, see Edward Brown, *The Proletarian Episode in Russian Literature 1928–32* (Columbia, 1953); A. Olkhovsky, *Music Under the Soviets* (New York, 1955); N. Gorchakov, *The Theatre in Soviet Russia* (Columbia, 1957); J. Leyda, *Kino: A History of the Russian and Soviet Film* (London, 1960). On

Stakhanovism, there is a substantial monograph by A. Pasquier, *Le Stakhanovisme* (Paris, 1938); and good, brief treatments in the older *Soviet Labor and Industry* (London, 1942), by Leonard E. Hubbard; and the more recent *Industrial Workers in the U.S.S.R.* (London, 1967), edited by Robert Conquest, which should also be used along with Deutscher and Schwarz for the study of wages, hours, labor discipline, and trade unions. Soviet economic imperialism among the non-Russian nationalities of the Soviet Union is touched upon in the two works by Walter Kolarz, *Russia and Her Colonies* (London, 1952), and *Peoples of the Soviet Far East* (London, 1954). Expropriations and the exploitative trade relationships with Eastern European satellites after World War II are summarized in Victor Winston, "The Satellites—Economic Liability," *Problems of Communism* (Jan., 1958), 14–20. Surveys (and critiques) of Soviet planning can be found in Naum Jasny, *Essays on the Soviet Economy* (New York, 1962); Alexander Baykov, *The Development of the Soviet Economic System* (Cambridge, 1946); Robert W. Campbell, *Soviet Economic Power*, 2nd ed. (New York, 1966); and Alec Nove, *The Soviet Economy* (New York, 1961). For an excellent study of the early plan period, see E. Zaleski, *Planification de la croissance et fluctuations économiques en U.R.S.S.* (Paris, 1962). The most authoritative soviet history of planning is Ivan A. Gladkov, *Ot plana GOELRO k planu 6 pyatilyetki* (*From Plan GOELRO to the 6th Five Year Plan*), (Moscow, 1956). There is an English translation of the recent survey by I. A. Evenko, *Planning in the U.S.S.R.* (Moscow, 1962). A recent and perceptive study, based on extensive interviews with soviet planners, is Philippe J. Bernard, *Planning in the Soviet Union* (Oxford, 1966). The original version of the First Five Year Plan, *Gosplan, Pyatilyetnii plan narodnokhozyaistvennovo stroitel'stva S S S R*, 3rd ed. (Moscow, 1930), 3 vols., appears in an abbreviated English version, *The Soviet Union Looks Ahead: The Five Year Plan for Economic Reconstruction* (London, 1930). On soviet industrial administration, the key work is Joseph Berliner, *Factory and Manager in the U.S.S.R.* (Harvard, 1957).

On the relationship of science, technology, and technological education to the Stalinist industrialization drive, see Alexander Vucinich, *The Soviet Academy of Sciences* (Stanford, 1956); Loren Graham, *The Soviet Academy of Sciences and the Communist Party 1917–1932* (Princeton, 1967); George L. Kline, ed., *Soviet Education* (London, 1957); and George S. Counts, *The Challenge of Soviet Education* (New York, 1957). The work of foreign engineers and technologists in Russia during the 1930's is discussed in the article by G. Cleinow in Gerhard Dobbert, ed., *Red Economics* (Boston-New York, 1932), 270–90; and in more exaggerated terms, but with much more detail on the American contracts, in Werner Keller, *Are the Russians Ten Feet Tall?* (London, 1961). A list of contracting American firms at the beginning of the First Five Year Plan is included in the appendix to the English version of the plan.

Out of the substantial body of literature dealing with soviet statistics, two books present a good summary and analysis: Naum Jasny, *The Soviet 1956 Statistical Handbook* (Michigan State University Press, 1957); and Gregory Grossman, *Soviet Statistics of Physical Output* (Princeton, 1960). For a compact collection of official statistics, see *Strana Sovietov za 50 lyet* (*The Soviet Land for 50 Years*), (Moscow, 1967). The clearest and fullest exposition of soviet economic growth and of the literature which deals with it is Gilbert W. Nutter, *Growth of Industrial Production in the Soviet Union* (Princeton, 1962). One must also consult the older work by Naum Jasny, *The Soviet Economy in the Plan Era* (Stanford, 1951), as well as his more recent study of soviet industrialization mentioned earlier in this bibliography. Other interesting and important estimates which should be noted are Abram Bergson, *The Real National Income of the Soviet Union Since 1928* (Harvard, 1961); Donald Hodgman, *Soviet Industrial Production 1928–51* (Harvard, 1954); and Francis Seton, *The Tempo of Soviet Industrial Expansion* (1957).

On the development of specific industries, regions, and periods, see Demitri B. Shimkin, *Minerals: A Key to Soviet Power* (Harvard, 1953). The best economic history of soviet transportation is Holland Hunter, *Soviet Transportation Policy* (Harvard, 1957); and for more technical aspects of soviet railroad development, see John N. Westwood, *History of Russian Railways,* cited previously. An excellent general survey of soviet industry can be found in Theodore Shabad, *Geography of the U.S.S.R.* (London, 1951); and a recent regional study (of the east), Violet Conolly, *Beyond the Urals* (London, 1967). Population changes can be studied in Frank Lorimer, *The Population of the Soviet Union* (League of Nations, 1946). An old and a new soviet history of the economy during the Second World War are Nikolai Voznesensky, *War Economy of the U.S.S.R.* (Moscow, 1948) and Grigorii I. Shigalin, *Narodnoe khozyaistvo S S S R v period velikoi otechestvennoi voiny* (*The Peoples Economy of the U.S.S.R. in the Period of the Great Fatherland War*), (Moscow, 1960).

CHAPTER 5 / INDUSTRIALIZED RUSSIA

There are a number of economic textbooks and surveys which provide an excellent, detailed, technical coverage of recent developments in soviet industry. See, for example, Harry Schwartz, *Russia's Soviet Economy* (New York, 1958); Robert W. Campbell, *Soviet Economic Power,* 2nd ed. (Boston, 1966); and Alec Nove, *The Soviet Economy: An Introduction* (New York, 1961). Another good survey of the dynamics and flaws of the soviet industrial economy is H. Chambre, *Union Sovietique et développement économique* (Paris, 1967). Chambre also provides extensive treatment of the Central Asian nationalities. Peter Wiles, *The Political Economy of Communism,* writes of soviet development within the context of other communist economies.

Three studies which are more historical in their treatment of the period since 1953 are Alec Nove, *An Economic History of the U.S.S.R.,* mentioned previously; Harry Schwartz, *The Soviet Economy Since Stalin* (Philadelphia and New York, 1965); and Anatole G. Mazour, *Soviet Economic Development* (New York, 1967), the largest chapter of which is devoted to the post-Stalin period. Mazour's textbook includes a selection of translated documents. An important and interesting primary source for recent soviet grass roots industrial history is the *Current Digest of the Soviet Press.*

Several important monographs, articles, and anthologies that have appeared recently should also be consulted. See Naum Jasny's informative study, *Khrushchev's Crop Policy* (Glasgow, 1965); Alec Nove's collection, *Economic Rationality and Soviet Politics* (New York, 1964); Margaret Miller's *Rise of the Russian Consumer* (London, 1965); Herbert S. Levine, "Industry," in Allen Kassof, ed., *Prospects for Soviet Society* (London, 1968); Stanley Cohn, "The Soviet Economy: Performance and Growth"; and James H. Blackman, "The Kosygin Reforms: New Wine in Old Bottles?" in Vladimir G. Treml, ed., *The Development of the Soviet Economy* (New York, 1968).

Index